INTERNATIONAL DEVELOPMENT IN FOCUS

Enhancing STEM Education and Careers in Sri Lanka

SHALIKA SUBASINGHE, SHOBHANA SOSALE, AND HARSHA ATURUPANE

WORLD BANK GROUP

Contents

Figures

Maps

Tables

Acknowledgments

The authors wish to thank our World Bank colleagues Lynne Sherburne-Benz and Cristian Aedo for their valuable guidance during the preparation of this report. The authors also thank Anna Fruttero and Yoko Nagashima who served as peer reviewers, and Gunjan Gautam, Maria Beatriz Orlando, Yukari Shibuya, and Pranav Vaidya, from the South Asia Regional Infrastructure and Social Development Practice Groups, for their collaboration.

The authors thank the Ministry of Education (formerly the Ministry of Education [school education]; the State Ministry of Skills Development, Vocational Education, Research & Innovation; the State Ministry of Higher Education; and the former Ministry of Science and Technology for facilitating the preparation of the study and sharing their insights regarding STEM education in Sri Lanka.

The authors also wish to thank the following experts for their guidance and support: Padmini Ranaweera, Chandana Udawatte, Haritha Abeytunga, Nimalakith Samarakoon, Kumudika Boyagoda, Upul Sonnadara, Mahen Muttaiah, Gominda Ponnamperuma, and Kamani Jayasekera.

Paul Holtz and Ann O'Malley edited the report. This report is associated with "South Asia Human Capital Analysis II," a World Bank white paper completed in June 2022.

About the Authors

Harsha Aturupane is a lead economist at the World Bank. He has also been the country sector coordinator for human development for Sri Lanka and the Maldives, and the program leader for human development for the Maldives, Nepal, and Sri Lanka, at the World Bank. He has worked and written extensively in the fields of human development, education economics, higher education, general education, labor economics, welfare economics, and the economics of inequality and poverty reduction. He has led teams in the preparation and supervision of World Bank projects and programs covering higher education, general education, health, social protection, economic reform, private sector development, and governance processes. He has a PhD and MPhil in economics from the University of Cambridge and a BA in economics and diploma in economic development from the University of Colombo.

Shobhana Sosale is a senior education specialist in the South Asia Region of the World Bank Education Global Practice. She is global co-lead for the education and gender thematic area and is the climate change and education focal point for South Asia. She has more than 25 years of experience in education and skills development. She has published on topics in education and related fields, analyzing topics linking political economy and cross-sectoral issues in education, technology, climate change, skills development, entrepreneurship, public partnerships, and finance. She has led the World Bank's education engagement in more than 14 countries in East Asia, Europe and Central Asia, the Middle East and North America, South Asia, and Sub-Saharan Africa. She also has academic teaching experience at the graduate and undergraduate levels. She holds graduate degrees in political economy and macroeconomics.

Shalika Subasinghe is a consultant working with the World Bank Education Global Practice and Social Protection & Jobs Global Practice in the South Asia Region. Her most recent work focuses on projects and analytical work relating to early childhood development, skills development, jobs, demographic transition, public expenditure reviews, and social safety nets in Sri Lanka, and pension and social protection in the Maldives. Previously, she has published in the fields of marketing, consumer behavior, and education. Prior to joining the World

Bank, she worked for Distance Learning Center Ltd, the Sri Lankan node of the World Bank's Global Development Learning Network, as the learning and development manager, as well as in several universities in Australia and Sri Lanka where she lectured at the undergraduate and postgraduate levels. She is a Fulbright Scholar and holds a master's in business administration from the University of New Hampshire (United States), a graduate certificate in university teaching and learning from Charles Sturt University (Australia), and a bachelor of commerce from the University of Colombo (Sri Lanka).

Executive Summary

Science, technology, engineering, and mathematics (STEM) are crucial fields for economic development and social inclusion—making it essential that Sri Lanka increase access to and participation in STEM education and careers, especially for girls. STEM skills and experiences, coupled with a diversity of perspectives, are integral to building the STEM workforce in Sri Lanka. Inclusion and diversity must be championed by the government and STEM stakeholders.

Policies for education and other sectors have highlighted the crucial role of education in economic development. During the early twenty-first century, the government introduced reforms aimed at enhancing education access and quality as well as emphasizing the importance of science, mathematics, and technology. Numerous initiatives have been introduced to boost demand for general education, which encompasses the primary (grades 1–5), lower secondary (grades 6–9), upper secondary (grades 10–11), and collegiate (grades 12–13) levels. In addition, in 2017, the government made 13 years of education compulsory, keeping students in school by introducing a vocational stream for those who do not qualify for other subject streams.

In 2020, Sri Lanka had 10,155 public primary and secondary schools, 90 private schools, 30 special schools, and 816 state-funded and state-managed *pirivenas* (temple schools). In 2020, student enrollment was 4.06 million in public schools, 136,230 in private schools, 2,496 in special schools, and 69,878 in *pirivenas*. In public schools, females accounted for 49 percent of enrollments at the primary level, 50 percent at the secondary level, and 55 percent at the collegiate level. Girls have slightly lower repetition and dropout rates, and they attend and remain in school at slightly higher rates.

Although STEM stands for science, technology, engineering, and mathematics, none of the four subjects are available for continuous learning from the primary to collegiate levels for all students. Mathematics is a required subject from grades 1–11. At the lower secondary level, mathematics, science, and practical technical skills are compulsory subjects. In some schools, information and communications technology (ICT) is offered as a subject in grades 1–9 or 6–9. At the upper secondary level, in addition to compulsory classes in science and mathematics, students can study other optional STEM subjects if they are offered at their school.

The seeds of STEM education must be planted in grade 1. Activities conducted in preschool to develop curiosity, problem-solving, critical thinking, numeracy, and writing skills are incorporated into subjects such as mathematics, environmental studies, and languages (English, Sinhala, and Tamil) at the primary level. Assessments of mathematics learning in grades 4 and 5 scholarship examinations reveal higher scores for girls.

After primary school, classes in science, practical technical skills, and health science are introduced. Most schools with computer labs offer ICT as a subject starting in grade 6. By grade 8, girls outperform boys in mathematics and science, with failure rates falling for girls but rising for boys. In addition, 76 percent of girls (compared with 58 percent of boys) passed the General Certificate of Education (GCE) Ordinary Level (O/L), qualifying them to continue to the GCE Advanced Level (A/L). Again, girls did better than boys on mathematics and science.

Upon completing the GCE O/L, students move to the collegiate level. STEM streams include physical science and bioscience for science and biotechnology and engineering technology for technology. Although girls outperform boys in mathematics and science from grade 4 through the GCE O/L, nearly three-fourths of girls pursue non-STEM streams for the GCE A/L.

Once they have finished 13 years of education, students sit for the GCE A/L to qualify for higher education. Among selected STEM subjects, overall student performance was highest in biology and lowest in combined mathematics. The trend was similar for girls, with the best performance in biology and the worst in combined mathematics—although both were still higher than the average. Larger shares of boys passed physics and chemistry, but only about 32 percent of girls took the combined mathematics examination and 34 percent the chemistry examination.

In Sri Lanka's complex system for technical and vocational education and training (TVET), female enrollment as a share of the total rose from 40 percent in 2016 to 49 percent in 2021. In addition, women are increasingly engaged in STEM-related TVET, with such enrollments jumping 105 percent between 2016 and 2021.

In higher education, 128,188 students were enrolled in 15 state universities in 2019. Of those, 49 percent (22 percent male and 27 percent female) took STEM courses. More female undergraduates in state universities are taking STEM courses. Between 2011 and 2021, the number of graduates from state universities in STEM subjects jumped 39 percent. Nonstate higher education institutions also contribute to undergraduate STEM output. In addition, women accounted for 41 percent of postgraduate STEM degrees in 2015, 46 percent in 2019, and 52 percent in 2021.

In 2019, the labor force in Sri Lanka consisted of 8.1 million workers, only 34 percent of whom were female. Around 45 percent of workers—one-third of them women—were engaged in STEM-related occupations. Graduates of state higher education institutions are more likely to be employed, and employed more quickly, if they hold STEM degrees.

Numerous factors enable and prevent women's access to STEM education and careers in Sri Lanka. These include macroeconomic conditions; the country's poverty profile; policy, governance, quality, and financial issues for school education; TVET, higher education, and labor market participation; and socio-cultural factors. The policy on expanding access to STEM education will be achieved by creating new university departments and expanding faculties for

STEM courses. Women's participation in the STEM labor force can be increased with help from professional organizations and programs to attract and retain female workers (especially after childbirth), among other efforts.

At the primary level, schools need to be fully functioning so that all students can attend and acquire the foundational knowledge and skills needed for STEM education. All primary schools need to have trained, qualified teachers focused on children's learning outcomes in subjects such as mathematics and the environment—with support from parents and the government. Over the medium to long term, needy children in remote locations will require assistance that enhances school access and quality.

At the secondary level, schools need to provide inclusive access to students, including underprivileged ones. Teachers qualified and trained in science, mathematics, and practical and technical skills are needed in all secondary schools, as are facilities such as science and computer labs to offer science, mathematics, ICT, and other technology subjects. Assessments of science and mathematics knowledge among eighth-grade students should guide decisions that strengthen learning outcomes and support career guidance programs.

At the collegiate level, more schools need to offer science and technology courses or vocational streams geared toward STEM. Curricula for bioscience, physical science, and technology subjects need to be reviewed to ensure that they provide the knowledge and skills needed for students to pursue higher studies or join the workforce. Career guidance programs need to be offered to highlight options for continued study and the labor market, and facilities—such as buildings and labs—must be developed.

Among TVET institutions, more students need to be enrolled in STEM areas in public TVET institutions. Female students must be encouraged to pursue stipends. Industry collaborations need to be facilitated for apprenticeships, on-the-job training, teacher training, product designs, and innovations in STEM fields. Awareness sessions should be held for students, parents, and communities to promote female role models and job opportunities.

Higher education institutions need to increase the number of students enrolled in STEM courses by renovating buildings or increasing the use of infrastructure facilities. Such institutions need to also revise curricula to integrate content relevant to the world of work, enhance links between universities and industry, and offer career guidance. In addition, efforts need to be made to enhance funding of state and nonstate universities to increase STEM access and quality, as well as to develop business links between universities and global businesses or foreign universities to strengthen research and innovation.

In the labor market, female role models need to be promoted, including through the media, to encourage schoolchildren and postsecondary students to pursue STEM. Employers must be encouraged to recruit female workers and develop family- and female-friendly benefits and policies. Continuous development programs need to be developed to acquire or enhance STEM skills in the workplace and advance careers. Finally, in the medium to long term, labor market policies and laws need to be made more female-friendly, with equal wages for occupations requiring the same knowledge, skills, and abilities.

Abbreviations

A/L	Advanced Level
BPM	business process management firm
CEB	Ceylon Electricity Board
CGTTI	Ceylon German Technical Training Institute
DCS	Department of Census & Statistics
DTET	Department of Technical Education & Training
EAP	East Asia and Pacific
ESMAP	Energy Sector Management Assistance Program
GAR	gross attendance ratio
GCE	General Certificate of Education
GDP	gross domestic product
HSS	humanities and social science
ICT	information and communications technology
IT	information technology
MoE	Ministry of Education
NAITA	National Apprentice Industrial Training Authority
NAR	net attendance rate
NASTEC	National Science and Technology Commission
NEC	National Education Commission
NVQ	National Vocational Qualification
NYSC	National Youth Services Council
OCUSL	Ocean University of Sri Lanka
O/L	Ordinary Level
PG	postgraduate
SA	South Asia
SMSDVERI	State Ministry of Skills Development, Vocational Education, Research & Innovation
STEM	science, technology, engineering, and mathematics
TVET	technical and vocational education and training
UGC	University Grants Commission
UNIVOTEC	University of Vocational Technology
VTA	Vocational Training Authority

1 Introduction

ABOUT THE REPORT

This report presents the landscape for science, technology, engineering, and mathematics (STEM) education and careers in Sri Lanka. It proposes education policies and STEM education status by gender at the central, provincial, and district levels; highlights factors enabling and hindering the achievement of desired outcomes; and offers policy options for decision-makers at the central and provincial levels to achieve the country's potential to expand human capital and contribute to economic development.

Sri Lanka's education system has undergone many reforms, with not all focusing on the promotion of specific subject areas. During the early twenty-first century, the government developed a sectorwide policy approach that emphasized the importance of science, mathematics, and technology in education development frameworks and programs (Aturupane and Little 2020). These programs aimed to enhance education access and quality.

Policies for education and other sectors have highlighted the crucial role of education in economic development. In the 2008 National Science and Technology Policy, science and technology play a key role in economic development, with education being essential in achieving it (National Science and Technology Commission [NASTEC] 2008). Furthermore, in the 2018 National Science, Technology, and Innovation Policy (NASTEC 2018), equal access to science education for all schoolchildren is key for inclusive economic growth.

The National Education Policy Framework for 2020–30 highlights the pivotal role of science, technology, and innovation in enhancing competitiveness (National Education Commission [NEC] 2022). The framework highlights the need to encourage science, engineering, and allied fields to increase competitiveness and enhance opportunities for labor force participation. It also calls for a multipronged approach in improving access to science and mathematics education, enhancing the quality of teachers and infrastructure, and increasing the relevance of education to strengthen opportunities for gainful employment.

GENERAL EDUCATION LANDSCAPE

Sri Lanka has a complex education system, and numerous policy initiatives have been introduced to increase demand for general education. These efforts include providing the following:

- Free education and textbooks in public schools
- Materials for making school uniforms (or vouchers to buy such materials) for all children every year
- Subsidized public transport for schoolchildren, including bus and train tickets
- Shoes for schoolchildren from vulnerable areas
- Scholarships for students who pass the grade 5 scholarship examination

In 2017, the government required 13 years of compulsory education, keeping students in school by introducing a vocational stream for those who do not qualify for other subject streams.

The Ministry of Education (MoE) is responsible for Sri Lanka's 373 national schools, while the Ministry of Provincial Councils covers 9,782 provincial ones (MoE 2020). The MoE provides policy guidance to state and private schools that use local syllabi; it does not govern international schools. The ministry also oversees central agencies involved in education, such as the National Institute of Education, Department of Examination, Directorate of Education, Colleges of Education, and Teachers Colleges. The NEC offers recommendations to the president on education policies and generates proposals for the education sector. The commission, which is expected to coordinate the growth of education policies with stakeholder agencies, developed the Educational Policy Framework for 2020–30. The National Policy on Education guides efforts to improve the quality of education (NEC 2016).

General education encompasses the primary, lower secondary, upper secondary, and collegiate levels. Primary education covers grades 1–5; lower secondary, grades 6–9; upper secondary, grades 10–11; and the collegiate level, grades 12–13. Until 2017, access to the collegiate level required passing the General Certificate of Education (GCE) Ordinary Level (O/L) examination, but since the introduction of 13 years of compulsory education, students who do not pass that examination can continue their studies by selecting a vocational stream. Schools have developed criteria for such students seeking to study STEM.

In 2020, Sri Lanka had 10,155 public primary and secondary schools, 90 private schools, 30 special schools, and 816 state-funded and state-managed *pirivenas* (temple schools). The central province had the most public schools (1,518, or 14.9 percent of the total; map 1.1), followed by the western province (1,355; 13.3 percent). The north-central province had the fewest public schools (815; 8.0 percent), followed by the Uva province (896; 8.8 percent).

Public schools are classified into four categories indicating the subject streams available:

- Type 1AB schools offer science classes (physical science, bioscience, or both) for the GCE Advanced Level (A/L).
- Type 1C schools offer A/L classes other than science (arts, commerce, and/or technology, and/or vocational).
- Type 2 schools offer classes through grade 11 (grades 1–11 or grades 6–11).
- Type 3 schools offer classes from grades 1–5 or grades 1–8 (MoE 2020).

MAP 1.1

Distribution of public schools in Sri Lanka, by province, 2020

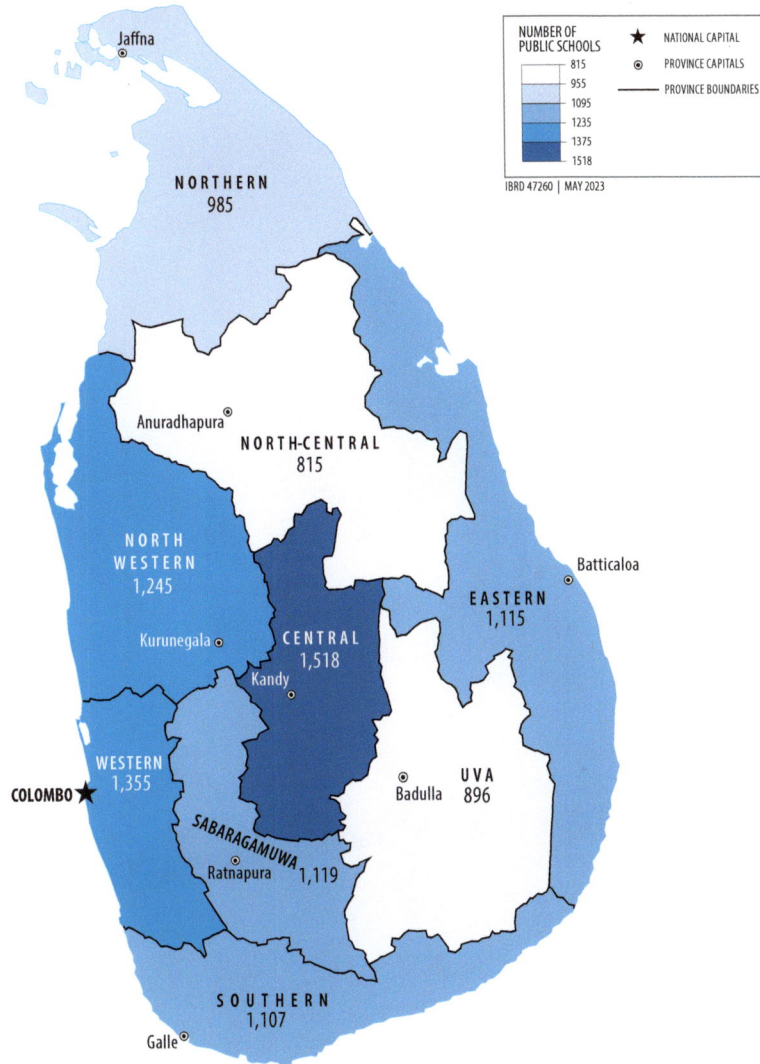

NUMBER OF PUBLIC SCHOOLS		★ NATIONAL CAPITAL
815		◉ PROVINCE CAPITALS
955		─── PROVINCE BOUNDARIES
1095		
1235		
1375		
1518		

IBRD 47260 | MAY 2023

Source: Ministry of Education 2020.

Efforts to increase the number of students pursuing science, mathematics, and technology at the collegiate level are constrained by the number of schools in each category. In 2020, there were 1,000 type 1AB schools (10 percent of all schools), 1,932 type 1C schools (19 percent), and 3,224 type 2 schools (32 percent). Type 3 schools accounted for the remaining 39 percent. The distribution of subject offerings sheds light on opportunities for students to pursue subjects at the collegiate level. Physical science was offered in 920 schools (92 percent of type 1AB schools), bioscience in 912 (91 percent of type 1AB schools), technology in 512, biotechnology in 486, and engineering technology in 448 (MoE 2020).

The distribution of school types varies by province. In 2020, the western province had the most type 1AB schools (187; map 1.2) and the central province the most type 1C schools (323). The north-central province had the fewest type 1AB schools (61), while the northern province had the fewest type 1C schools (129).

MAP 1.2
Distribution of type 1AB and type 1C schools in Sri Lanka, by province, 2020

a. Type 1AB Schools

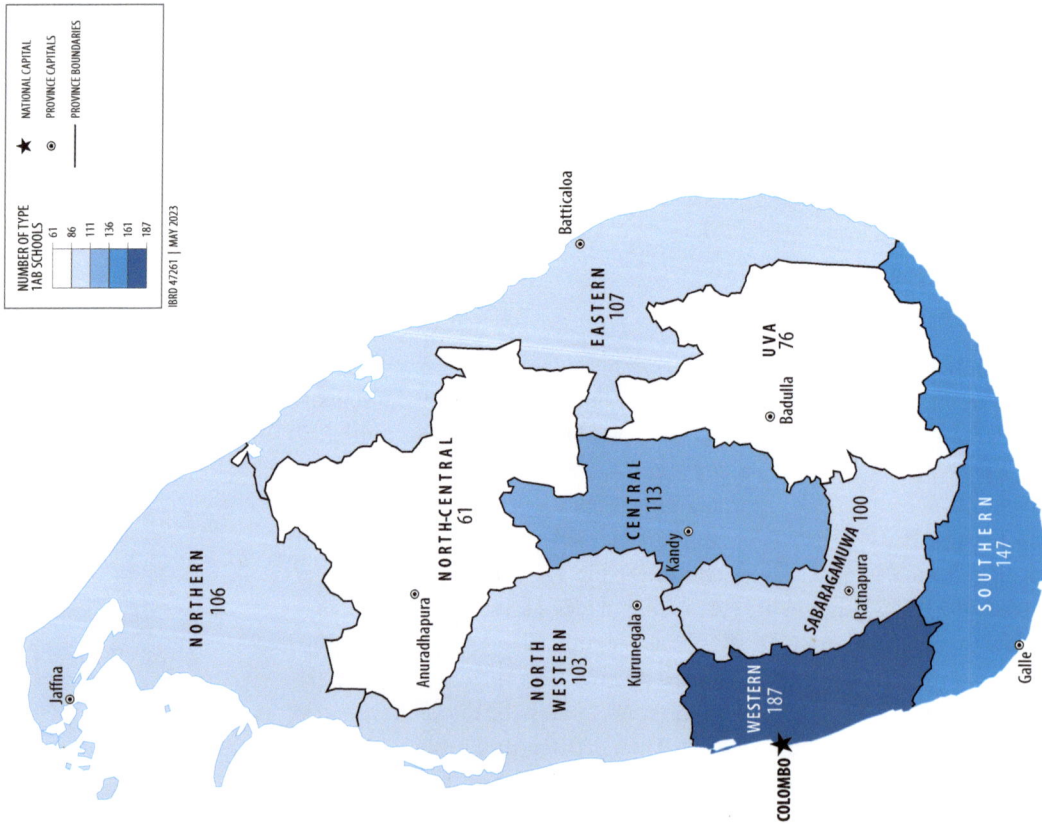

NUMBER OF TYPE
1AB SCHOOLS
61
86
111
136
161
187

NATIONAL CAPITAL
PROVINCE CAPITALS
PROVINCE BOUNDARIES

IBRD 47261 | MAY 2023

Jaffna

NORTHERN
106

Anuradhapura

NORTH-CENTRAL
61

NORTH
WESTERN
103

Kurunegala

CENTRAL
113

Kandy

EASTERN
107

Batticaloa

UVA
76

Badulla

WESTERN
187

COLOMBO

SABARAGAMUWA
100

Ratnapura

SOUTHERN
147

Galle

b. Type 1C Schools

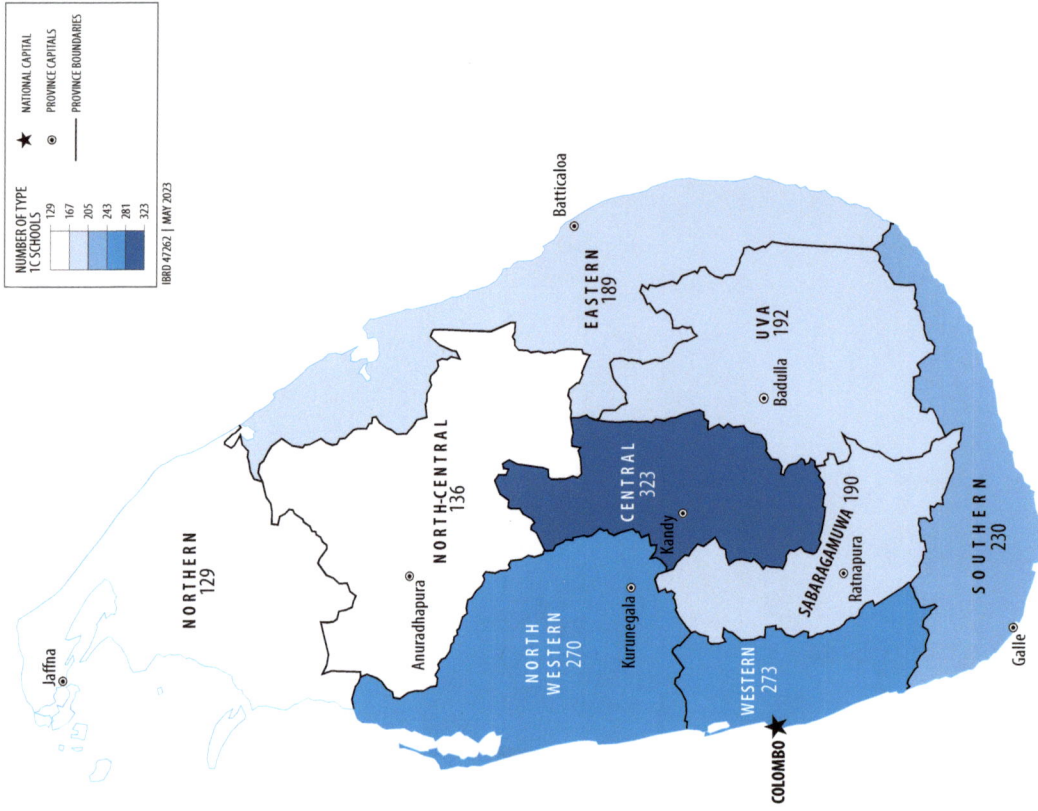

NUMBER OF TYPE
1C SCHOOLS
129
167
205
243
281
323

NATIONAL CAPITAL
PROVINCE CAPITALS
PROVINCE BOUNDARIES

IBRD 47262 | MAY 2023

Jaffna

NORTHERN
129

Anuradhapura

NORTH-CENTRAL
136

NORTH
WESTERN
270

Kurunegala

CENTRAL
323

Kandy

EASTERN
189

Batticaloa

UVA
192

Badulla

WESTERN
273

COLOMBO

SABARAGAMUWA
190

Ratnapura

SOUTHERN
230

Galle

Source: Ministry of Education 2020.

Enrollments vary by province and school type. In 2020, student enrollment was 4.06 million in public schools, 136,230 in private schools, 2,496 in special schools, and 69,878 in *pirivenas*, with around 23 percent of students in the western province, followed by 12 percent in the northwestern province (table 1.1). Less than 6 percent of students were in the northern province. Schools in the western province had an average of 685 students, compared with 227 in the northern province. Among public schools, 38.7 percent of students (1.57 million) attended type 1AB schools, 26.0 percent (1.08 million) type 1C schools, 18.5 percent type 2 schools, and 16.4 percent type 3 schools. The average number of students in type 1AB schools ranged from 2,300 in the western province to 827 in the northern province. Around 27 percent of Sri Lankan students in type 1AB schools were in the western province, compared with 6 percent in the northern, north-central, and Uva provinces. Furthermore, 21 percent of students enrolled in type 1C schools were in the western province, compared with 4 percent in the northern province.

Gender differences are evident in public and private school enrollments. In public schools in 2020, females accounted for 49 percent of enrollments at the primary level, 50 percent at the secondary level, and 55 percent at the collegiate level (table 1.2). Higher female enrollments at the collegiate level could be due to boys dropping out of school. In private schools, female enrollments were lower at the primary and secondary levels but higher at the collegiate level.

Slight gender disparities exist in the net attendance rate (NAR) at primary and secondary schools in Sri Lanka. The NAR for primary school is the percentage of primary school-age children (five- to nine-year-olds) attending primary school at the right level for their age. In 2016, the NAR at the primary level was 97.9 percent (97.8 percent for boys and 98.1 percent for girls; Department of Census & Statistics [DCS] 2017). The lowest NAR for girls was in the Mullativu district (87.3 percent for girls and 94.4 percent for boys). The NAR for the lowest quintile was also lower for girls (96.6 percent) than for boys (97.5 percent). The NAR also measures school attendance of secondary school-age children (10- to 15-year-olds). Although the aggregate NAR for Sri Lanka does not show a difference between genders, with both at 83.1 percent, there were differences among districts. In some districts, the NAR was higher for girls, including in Puttlam (75.5 percent for boys and 80.0 percent for girls), Monaragala (77.5 percent for boys and 88.4 percent for girls), and Mullativu (79.5 percent for boys and 87.7 percent for girls). In other districts, the NAR was lower for girls, including Ampara (87.3 percent for boys and 75.6 percent for girls) and Nuwara Eliya (83.6 percent for boys and 79.4 percent for girls). The NAR for the lowest quintile was 83.1 percent for girls and 80.4 percent for boys—indicating that boys from this quintile drop out more than girls.

Girls have slightly lower repetition rates. Most schools automatically promote students from one grade to the next, but if children have not achieved the required competencies, most schools recommend that they remain in the same grade instead of moving to the next one. The repetition rate represents the number of repeaters in a given grade each year, presented as a percentage of enrollment in that grade in the previous school year. In 2017, the repetition rate was 1.03 percent for boys and 0.88 percent for girls in grade 5 (MoE 2017).

Boys tend to drop out more, with the dropout rate representing the proportion of students from a cohort enrolled in a given grade for a given school year who are no longer enrolled in the following grade. In grade 10, the student dropout rate was 4.6 percent for boys and 2.8 percent for girls (MoE 2017).

TABLE 1.1 **School enrollment in Sri Lanka, by province and public school type, 2020**

PROVINCE	TOTAL				TYPE 1AB SCHOOLS				TYPE 1C SCHOOLS			
	SCHOOLS	STUDENTS	STUDENTS (%)	AVERAGE NUMBER OF STUDENTS PER SCHOOL	SCHOOLS	STUDENTS	STUDENTS (%)	AVERAGE NUMBER OF STUDENTS	SCHOOLS	STUDENTS	STUDENTS (%)	AVERAGE NUMBER OF STUDENTS
Central	1,518	537,973	13	354	113	176,424	11	1,561	323	169,656	16	525
Eastern	1,115	378,841	9	340	107	126,244	8	1,180	189	98,132	9	519
North-central	815	297,731	7	365	61	97,974	6	1,606	136	77,075	7	567
Northern	985	223,333	5	227	106	87,676	6	827	129	42,898	4	333
Northwestern	1,245	503,153	12	404	103	176,427	11	1,713	270	156,411	15	579
Sabaragamuwa	1,119	389,557	10	348	100	144,352	9	1,444	190	94,491	9	497
Southern	1,107	517,397	13	467	147	237,389	15	1,615	230	122,078	11	531
Uva	896	287,823	7	321	76	93,970	6	1,236	192	87,038	8	453
Western	1,355	927,877	23	685	187	430,184	27	2,300	273	228,850	21	838
Total	**10,155**	**4,063,685**	**100**	**400**	**1,000**	**1,570,640**	**100**	**1,571**	**1,932**	**1,076,629**	**100**	**557**

Source: Ministry of Education 2020.

TABLE 1.2 **Male and female enrollments in public and private schools in Sri Lanka, by education level, 2020**

LEVEL	TOTAL	MALE	FEMALE	MALE (%)	FEMALE (%)
Public schools					
Primary	1,640,647	830,358	810,289	51	49
Secondary (grades 6–11)	1,994,422	995,430	998,992	50	50
Collegiate (grades 12–13)	421,114	187,804	233,310	45	55
Total	**4,056,183**	**2,013,592**	**2,042,591**	**50**	**50**
Private schools					
Primary	54,076	27,963	26,113	52	48
Secondary (grades 6–11)	64,608	33,947	30,661	53	47
Collegiate (grades 12–13)	17,546	8,581	8,965	49	51
Total	**136,230**	**70,491**	**65,739**	**52**	**48**

Source: Ministry of Education 2020.

The dropout rate for girls was highest in the Ampara and Trincomalee districts, both in the eastern province.

Girls tend to remain longer at school. The rate at which they remain in school longer is the percentage of a cohort of students in the first grade of a given cycle of education in a given school year who are expected to reach a given grade, regardless of repetition. In 2017, this rate in grade 5 was 98.67 percent (98.17 percent for boys and 99.18 percent for girls), but by grade 11, it fell to 88.75 percent (86.54 percent for boys and 91.03 percent for girls). The rate at which children remain in school longer was lowest in the eastern province and highest in the western province (MoE 2017).

The gross attendance ratio (GAR) shows a slight gender disparity among primary school children and a wider variation at the secondary level. The GAR measures participation at each school level among people between ages 6 and 15—including students who have repeated, dropouts who have returned, and those younger than the official age. In 2016, the GAR in Sri Lanka at the primary level was 100.8 percent (100.5 percent for boys and 101.4 percent for girls; DCS 2017). Among districts, the lowest GAR for boys was in Hambantota (96.8 percent; 100.1 percent for girls), while the lowest GAR for girls was in Mullativu (91.8 percent; 105.8 percent for boys). Even in the lowest quintile, the GAR for both genders was more than 100 percent (102.7 percent for boys and 100.9 percent for girls). At the secondary level, the difference between genders in the GAR was negligible (84.3 percent for boys and 84.5 percent for girls), but variations occurred across districts, with Monaragala having the lowest GAR for boys (77.5 percent) and Puttlam the lowest for girls (89.4 percent).

Teacher numbers vary by school type and province. In 2020, Sri Lanka had 249,494 teachers in public schools, 8,019 in private schools, 545 in special schools, and 7,136 in *pirivenas* (MoE 2020). Among public school teachers, 82,244 (33 percent) were in type 1AB schools, 67,837 (27 percent) in type 1C schools, 61,728 (25 percent) in type 2 schools, and 37,685 (15 percent) in type 3 schools. The largest share of these teachers (18.5 percent) worked in the western province and the smallest (7 percent) in the north-central province (table 1.3). The average public school had 24 teachers—although type 1AB schools had an average of 82.

TABLE 1.3 Number of and student ratios for public school teachers in Sri Lanka, by province, 2020

PROVINCE	TEACHERS	TEACHERS (%)	AVERAGE NUMBER TEACHERS PER SCHOOL						STUDENT/TEACHER RATIO					
			TOTAL	TYPE 1AB SCHOOL	TYPE 1C SCHOOL	TYPE 2 SCHOOL	TYPE 3 SCHOOL		TOTAL	TYPE 1AB SCHOOL	TYPE 1C SCHOOL	TYPE 2 SCHOOL	TYPE 3 SCHOOL
Central	35,067	14.1	23.1	85	34.5	18.8	9.1		15.3	18.27	15.2	11.5	16.5
Eastern	24,005	9.6	21.8	69	32.7	18.9	8.2		15.8	17.22	15.9	13.6	16.6
North-central	17,387	7.0	21.2	79	34.7	18.6	9.5		17.1	20.36	16.3	13.2	18.3
Northern	18,724	7.5	19.1	59	29.7	19.0	6.7		11.9	13.92	11.2	9.6	13.0
Northwestern	29,866	12.0	23.5	88	34.1	17.8	9.3		16.8	19.52	17.0	13.0	17.5
Sabaragamuwa	26,006	10.4	22.5	81	33.2	18.5	9.2		15.0	17.87	15.0	11.2	16.8
Southern	31,504	12.6	27.6	81	35.8	20.8	11.4		16.4	19.82	14.8	10.3	19.1
Uva	20,796	8.3	22.4	72	33.8	18.7	10.0		13.8	17.23	13.4	10.1	15.4
Western	46,139	18.5	33.8	105	42.9	21.1	12.1		20.1	21.95	19.5	15.5	22.7
Total	**249,494**	**100.0**	**24.3**	**82**	**35.1**	**19.1**	**9.4**		**16.3**	**19.10**	**15.9**	**12.2**	**17.7**

Source: Ministry of Education 2020.

Student/teacher ratios also differ by school type and province, averaging 16.3 at the national level, 19.1 in type 1AB schools, 15.9 in type 1C schools, 12.2 in type 2 schools, and 17.7 in type 3 schools (table 1.3). The northern province had the lowest student/teacher ratio (11.9)—meaning teachers had smaller workloads and greater availability to focus on student learning—while the western province had the highest (20.1).

REFERENCES

Aturupane, Harsha, and Angela W. Little. 2020. "General Education in Sri Lanka." In *Handbook of Education Systems in South Asia*, edited by P. M. Sarangapani and R. Pappu, 665–95. Singapore: Springer Singapore. https://doi.org/10.1007/978-981-13-3309-5_18-1.

Department of Census & Statistics (DCS) and Ministry of Health, Nutrition and Indigenous Medicine (MHNIM). 2017. *Sri Lanka Demographic and Health Survey 2016*. Colombo.

Ministry of Education. 2017. "Annual Performance Report." Colombo.

Ministry of Education. 2018. "Annual School Census." Columbo.

Ministry of Education. 2020. "Annual School Census." Columbo.

National Education Commission. 2016. "Proposals for a National Policy on General Education." Colombo.

National Education Commission. 2022. "National Education Policy Framework 2020–2030." Colombo.

National Science and Technology Commission. 2008. "National Science and Technology Policy." Colombo.

National Science and Technology Commission. 2018. "National Science, Technology, and Innovation Policy (draft)." Colombo.

2 STEM Education and Labor Market Landscape

STEM EDUCATION BY SCHOOL LEVEL

Although STEM stands for science, technology, engineering, and mathematics, none of the four subjects are available for continuous learning from the primary to collegiate levels for all students. Mathematics is a compulsory subject from grades 1–11. During primary school (grades 1–5), students take mathematics and environmental studies classes. Environmental studies provide foundational knowledge for subjects such as science, technology, and engineering in later years. At the lower secondary level (grades 6–9), mathematics, science, and practical technical skills are compulsory subjects. Teachers can also conduct activities to facilitate learning the foundational concepts of engineering and technology. In some schools, information and communications technology (ICT) is offered as a subject in grades 1–9 or grades 6–9.

UPPER SECONDARY LEVEL

At the upper secondary level (grades 10–11), in addition to compulsory classes in science and mathematics, students can study health and physical education, agriculture and food technology, ICT, aquatics biotechnology, design and construction technology, design and mechanical technology, and design and electrical and electronic technology if these optional subjects are offered at their school. Students must earn a credit pass or a simple pass to pursue physical science or bioscience streams. Students interested in the physical science stream can take combined mathematics, mathematics, or higher mathematics classes in grades 12–13, while most students in the bioscience stream take physics, chemistry, and biology classes. Students in the science, commerce, and arts streams can take ICT as an optional subject if it is offered at their school, while general information technology is compulsory.

PRIMARY LEVEL

The seeds of STEM education must be planted in grade 1. Activities conducted in preschool to develop curiosity, problem-solving, critical thinking, numeracy, and writing skills are incorporated into subjects such as mathematics, environmental studies, and languages (English, Sinhala, and Tamil) at the primary school level. Basic concepts of nature, environmental issues, and activity-based teaching are covered by co-curricular activities and assessed by a school-based system, but some type 2 and 3 schools focus more on preparing students for the grade 5 scholarship examination.

Assessments of mathematics learning of grade 4 students, conducted by the National Education Research and Evaluation Centre in various years (National Education Research and Evaluation Centre 2003, 2004, 2015), revealed differences by gender, province, and school type:

- In 2002, the average score was 37.9, with 39.0 for girls and 36.8 for boys. By 2015, the average score had jumped to 62.3, with 64.2 for girls and 60.1 for boys. Mathematics scores were closely correlated with reading comprehension (Anjum 2015). Most teachers use sentences to explain mathematics—and because girls have higher literacy skills, they can grasp and process complex concepts more easily.
- In 2015, students in the southern province had the highest average score (65.3) with a standard deviation of 20.56. Those in the eastern province had the lowest average score (56.1), as well as the highest standard deviation of 22.38 in scores, indicating more dispersion between the highest and lowest scores. The lowest standard deviation score of 19.72 was seen in the north-central province.
- In 2015, the average score was 67.7 in type 1AB schools and 64.2 in type 3 schools—above the national average of 62.3—compared with 60.0 in type 1C schools and 57.9 in type 2 schools. Type 2 schools offer classes from grades 1–11, while type 3 schools tend to have only primary-level classes. Thus, students in type 3 schools could be highly motivated to perform well.

Similarly, an assessment of grade 5 scholarship examination scores revealed gender and provincial variations among students who received scores above the cutoff mark. The examination assesses skills and abilities such as interpretation, prediction, reasoning, observation, problem-solving, and information organization. In 2021, across Sri Lanka, 16 percent of girls scored more than the cutoff mark of 70 or more, compared with 13 percent of boys (figure 2.1). Student performance was lowest in the central province for both girls (11 percent) and boys (10 percent). Girls performed best in the Sabaragamuwa province (18 percent), followed by the northwestern, north-central, and Uva (17 percent) provinces.

Students do not have to pass the grade 5 scholarship examination to continue to grade 6, but passing the examination helps students get into a national school (type 1AB). Because grade 5 scholarship examination scores help children gain access to a national or more popular school, parents and teachers encourage students to score high marks. There is also societal pressure on students to score high marks.

FIGURE 2.1

Students exceeding grade 5 scholarship examination cutoff of 70 marks or more in Sri Lanka, by gender and province, 2021

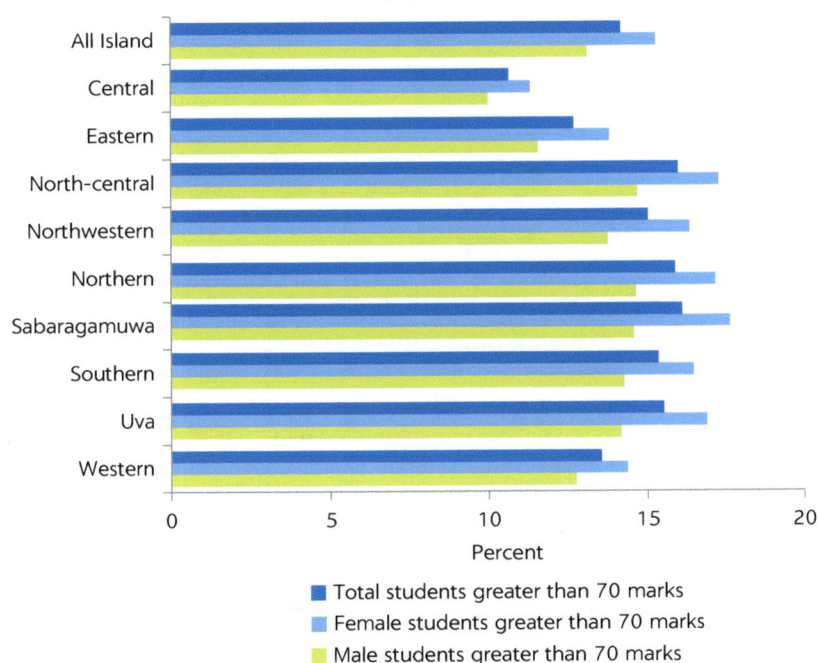

Source: Department of Examination 2021.

SECONDARY LEVEL

After primary school, students proceed to grade 6, where science, practical technical skills, and health science classes are introduced. Most schools with computer labs offer ICT as a subject starting in grade 6. Students are subjected to school-based or provincial-level assessments in grades 6 and 7. The National Education Research and Evaluation Centre has conducted national assessments of students in grade 8 to help decision-makers develop policies.

National assessments of learning outcomes in grade 8 reveal gender disparities. Assessments in 2012, 2014, and 2016 found that girls outperformed boys in mathematics and science (figure 2.2). In addition, girls' failure rates on examinations fell between 2012 and 2016 for both subjects—while boys' failure rates on examinations rose.

In 2016–17, the average national score for mathematics learning outcomes was 400, with 416 for girls and 383 for boys (figure 2.3). Scores were highest in the southern province and lowest in the eastern province. In all provinces, girls outperformed the average scores. Assessment outcomes for grade 8 scores in mathematics reveal gender and provincial variations.

Results from the examination for the General Certificate of Education (GCE) Ordinary Level (O/L) indicate gender and provincial differences. In 2015, 67.2 percent of students (76.0 percent of girls and 58.1 percent of boys; table 2.1) passed the GCE O/L—qualifying them to continue to the GCE Advanced Level (A/L). Students in the southern province were the most successful in passing the

FIGURE 2.2

National assessments of learning outcomes in grade 8 for mathematics and science in Sri Lanka, by gender, various years

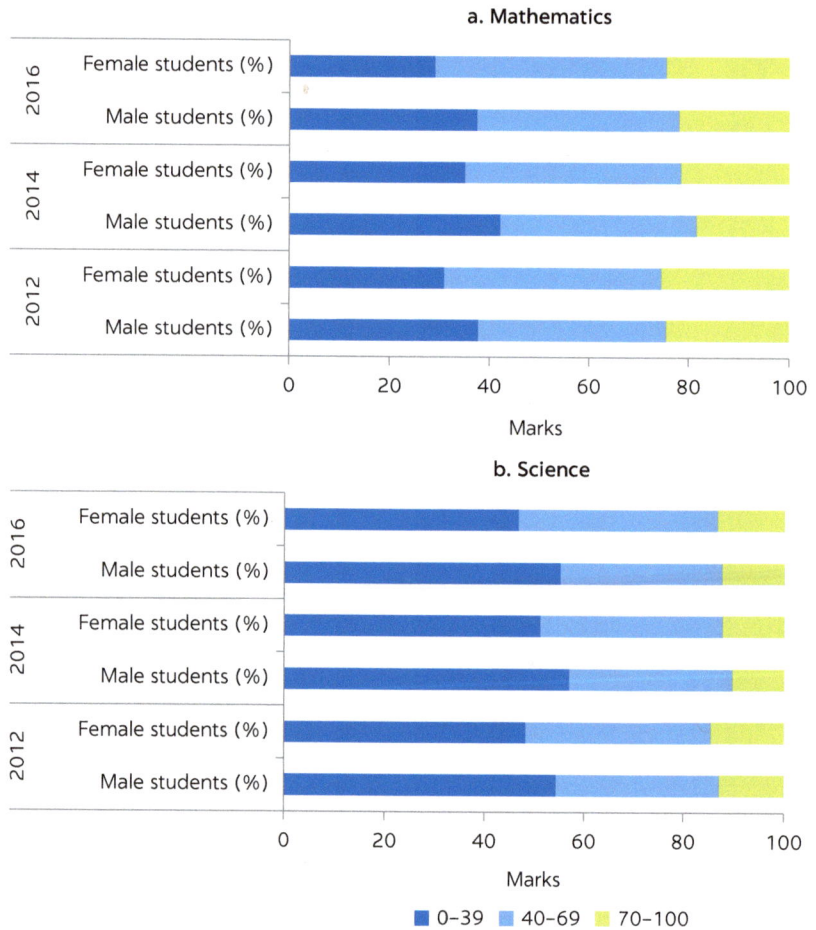

a. Mathematics

b. Science

■ 0–39 ■ 40–69 ■ 70–100

Sources: National Education Research and Evaluation Centre 2013, 2015, 2017.

FIGURE 2.3

Scores on mathematics learning outcomes in Sri Lanka, by province and gender, 2016–17

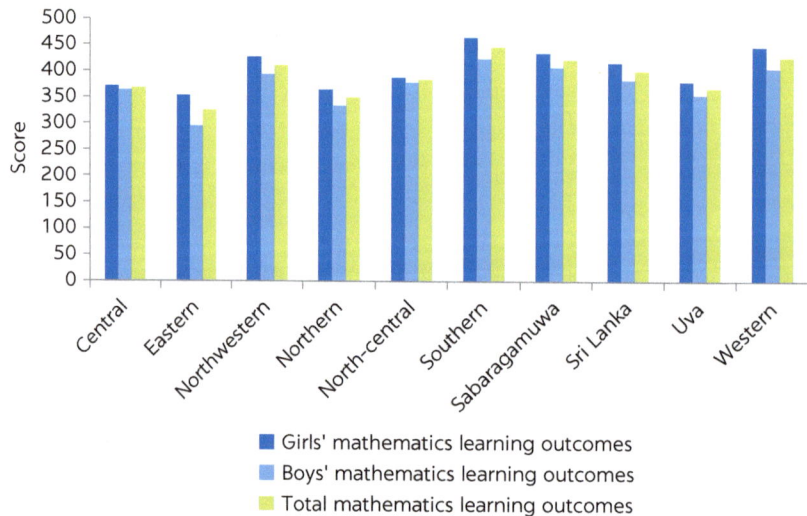

■ Girls' mathematics learning outcomes
■ Boys' mathematics learning outcomes
■ Total mathematics learning outcomes

Source: Aturupane et al. 2021.

TABLE 2.1 **Results of the general certificate examination ordinary level in Sri Lanka, by gender and province, 2015**

	TOTAL			MALE			FEMALE		
PROVINCE	**NUMBER TAKING GCE O/L**	**QUALIFIED FOR GCE A/L**		**NUMBER TAKING GCE O/L**	**QUALIFIED FOR GCE A/L**		**NUMBER TAKING GCE O/L**	**QUALIFIED FOR GCE A/L**	
		(n)	**(%)**		**(n)**	**(%)**		**(n)**	**(%)**
Central	37,557	24,134	64.26	18,531	10,126	54.64	19,026	14,008	73.63
Eastern	22,807	14,169	62.13	10,859	5,976	55.03	11,948	8,193	68.57
Northern	19,400	11,113	57.28	9,244	4,748	51.36	10,156	6,365	62.67
North-central	17,980	11,584	64.43	8,965	4,803	53.58	9,015	6,781	75.22
Northwestern	33,473	22,687	67.78	16,718	9,599	57.42	16,755	13,088	78.11
Sabaragamuwa	26,820	18,205	67.88	13,361	7,662	57.35	13,459	10,543	78.33
Southern	36,586	26,735	73.07	18,093	11,557	63.88	18,493	15,178	82.07
Uva	20,042	12,708	63.41	9,824	5,428	55.25	10,218	7,280	71.25
Western	76,264	54,023	70.84	38,595	23,892	61.9	37,669	30,131	79.99
Total	**290,929**	**195,358**	**67.15**	**144,190**	**83,791**	**58.11**	**146,739**	**111,567**	**76.03**

Source: Department of Examination 2015b.
Note: A/L = Advanced Level; GCE = General Certificate of Education; O/L = Ordinary Level.

TABLE 2.2 **Students passing the general certificate examination ordinary level in Sri Lanka, by gender and subject, 2015**

	TOTAL			MALE			FEMALE		
SUBJECT	**NUMBER TAKING EXAM**	**PASSED (n)**	**PASSED (%)**	**NUMBER TAKING EXAM**	**PASSED (n)**	**PASSED (%)**	**NUMBER TAKING EXAM**	**PASSED (n)**	**PASSED (%)**
Mathematics	340,057	176,580	51.9	166,750	78,860	47.3	173,307	97,720	56.4
Science	299,505	197,316	65.9	147,196	92,112	62.6	152,309	105,204	69.1

Source: Department of Examination 2015b.

GCE O/L (82.0 percent of girls and 63.9 percent of boys); those in the northern province were the least successful (62.7 percent for girls and 51.4 percent for boys). Since the government made 13 years of education compulsory in 2017, students who do not pass the GCE O/L can either repeat the examination the following year or continue in a vocational stream.

Mathematics and science results (table 2.2) for the GCE O/L indicate gender deviations. In 2015, 65.9 percent of students passed science (69.1 percent of girls and 62.6 percent of boys) and 51.9 percent passed mathematics (56.4 percent of girls and 47.3 percent of boys).

Optional subject offerings and enrollments vary. In addition to compulsory subjects for the GCE O/L, students can select three subjects from three groupings. In 2019, STEM-related optional subjects included ICT (54,577 students), agriculture and food technology (51,748 students), health and physical education (135,032 students), aquatic and biotechnology (729 students), design and construction technology (3,878 students), design and mechanical technology (3,230 students), and design and electrical and electronic technology (1,409 students) (Ministry of Education 2019).

COLLEGIATE LEVEL

After completing the GCE O/L, students move to the collegiate level. STEM streams are physical science and bioscience for science, as well as biotechnology and engineering technology for technology. Non-STEM streams include

TABLE 2.3 **Subject enrollment at the collegiate level in Sri Lanka, by gender, 2018 and 2020**

| | 2018 | | | | | | 2020 | | | | | |
| | TOTAL | | MALE | | FEMALE | | TOTAL | | MALE | | FEMALE | |
STREAM	(N)	(%)	(n)	(%)	(n)	(%)	(N)	(%)	(n)	(%)	(n)	(%)
STEM												
Bioscience	68,209	12	20,234	8	47,975	15	41,795	10	11,888	6	29,907	13
Biotechnology	25,364	4	10,858	4	14,506	5	—	—	—	—	—	—
Engineering technology	39,668	7	34,841	14	4,827	2	46,291	11	33,036	18	13,255	6
Physical science	64,623	11	41,654	17	22,969	7	47,328	11	28,996	15	18,332	8
Total	**197,864**	**35**	**107,587**	**43**	**90,277**	**28**	**135,414**	**32**	**73,920**	**39**	**61,494**	**26**
Non-STEM												
Arts	245,260	43	79,742	32	165,518	52	181,837	43	61,976	33	119,861	51
Commerce	120,075	21	57,968	23	62,107	19	90,243	21	43,481	23	46,762	20
Nonspecified/vocational	3,824	1	2,151	1	1,673	1	13,620	3	8427	4	5,193	2
Total	**369,159**	**65**	**139,861**	**57**	**229,298**	**72**	**285,700**	**68**	**113,884**	**61**	**171,816**	**74**
Total	**567,023**	**100**	**247,448**	**100**	**319,575**	**100**	**421,114**	**100**	**187,804**	**100**	**233,310**	**100**

Sources: Ministry of Education 2018, 2020.
Note: In 2020, the Ministry of Education reported student enrollment figures for the technology stream, which included biotechnology and engineering technology.

commerce, arts, and vocational studies. To pursue science or technology at the collegiate level, students must have passed the GCE O/L for science and mathematics.

Fewer students opt for STEM subjects at the collegiate level, with gender variations in enrollments. In 2020, 32 percent of enrolled students (39 percent of boys and 26 percent of girls) followed a STEM stream (table 2.3). Although girls outperform boys in mathematics and science from grade 4 through the GCE O/L, nearly three-quarters of girls pursue non-STEM streams for the GCE A/L. Moreover, most girls in a STEM stream enroll in bioscience (13 percent) or physical science (8 percent). Among girls, the least preferred streams are technology and vocational (2 percent each). Between 2018 and 2020, the number of students registering for STEM classes dropped.

After 13 years of education, students sit for the GCE A/L to qualify for higher education. The examination covers three subjects. The grades given are A (75–100 marks), B (65–74 marks), C (50–64 marks), S (35–49 marks), and F (34 and below). In 2020, more girls than boys passed all three subjects, obtained three As, passed two subjects, and passed one subject (figure 2.4), but girls also had a higher failure rate on examinations.

GCE A/L results reveal slight variations among provinces in the percentage of students who qualified to apply for university entrance. In 2015, the share of qualified students ranged from 59.6 percent in the north-central province to 64.9 percent in the Sabaragamuwa province (table 2.4). A similar difference could be seen in the share of qualified girls, ranging from 66.0 percent in the north-central province to 72.0 percent in the Sabaragamuwa province.

Among selected STEM subjects, overall student performance was highest in biology (with 73.5 percent passing) and lowest in combined mathematics (52.7 percent; table 2.5). The trend was similar for girls, with the best performance in biology (80.3 percent) and the worst in combined mathematics (59.8 percent). Larger shares of boys passed physics and chemistry.

FIGURE 2.4

General certificate examination advanced level results in Sri Lanka, by gender, 2014–20

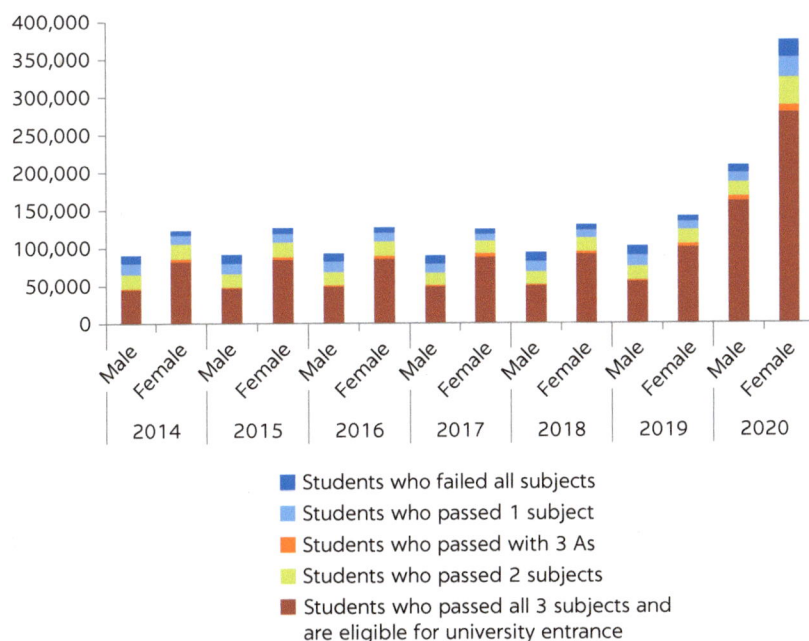

- Students who failed all subjects
- Students who passed 1 subject
- Students who passed with 3 As
- Students who passed 2 subjects
- Students who passed all 3 subjects and are eligible for university entrance

Sources: Department of Examination 2014, 2015a, 2016, 2017, 2018, 2019, 2020.

TABLE 2.4 **Students passing the general certificate examination advanced level in Sri Lanka, by gender and province, 2015**

PROVINCE	TOTAL		MALE		FEMALE	
	NUMBER TAKING EXAM	QUALIFIED (%)	NUMBER TAKING EXAM	QUALIFIED (%)	NUMBER TAKING EXAM	QUALIFIED (%)
Central	26,046	61.30	10,797	51.85	15,249	68.00
Eastern	24,032	60.15	10,200	49.22	13,832	68.21
Northern	14,658	61.69	6,185	51.30	8,473	69.28
North-central	11,910	59.56	4,984	50.62	6,926	66.00
Northwestern	12,684	65.23	5,316	56.72	7,368	71.38
Sabaragamuwa	20,451	64.88	8,225	54.37	12,226	71.95
Southern	29,945	62.34	12,222	52.95	17,723	68.82
Uva	14,093	62.81	5,753	52.32	8,340	70.05
Western	56,521	62.84	25,020	53.59	31,501	70.19
Total	**210,340**	**62.35**	**88,702**	**52.64**	**121,638**	**69.45**

Source: Department of Examination 2015a.

Moreover, only about 32 percent of girls took the combined mathematics examination and 34 percent the chemistry examination. More girls took the GCE A/L examination in economics (54 percent), business studies (52 percent), and accounting (52 percent), and more than 83 percent passed all three subjects. These three subjects belong to the commerce stream and are considered non-STEM. Students who follow the commerce stream tend to become accountants, bankers, and the like, opting to take professional examinations in accounting, finance, and banking without entering university.

TABLE 2.5 **General certificate examination advanced level results in selected subjects in Sri Lanka, by gender, 2015**

STREAM	TOTAL		MALE		FEMALE	
	NUMBER TAKING EXAM	PASSED (%)	NUMBER TAKING EXAM	PASSED (%)	NUMBER TAKING EXAM	PASSED (%)
STEM						
Biology	10,488	73.52	4,332	63.92	4,942	80.28
Chemistry	63,310	65.39	29,655	66.66	21,629	64.27
Combined mathematics	28,178	52.73	19,286	49.46	8,892	59.84
Physics	60,525	65.56	29,169	67.36	31,356	63.88
Non-STEM						
Accounting	53,481	74.47	25,523	65.11	27,958	83.02
Business studies	53,703	90.29	25,949	84.54	27,754	95.67
Economics	64,462	78.86	29,414	71.93	35,048	84.67
Political science	39,632	73.97	12,591	65.08	27,041	78.10

Source: Department of Examination 2015a.
Note: STEM = science, technology, engineering, and mathematics.

STEM-RELATED TECHNICAL AND VOCATIONAL EDUCATION AND TRAINING

Sri Lanka's system for technical and vocational education and training (TVET) is complex. The Tertiary and Vocational Education Commission, responsible for policy formulation, quality assurance, planning, development, and coordination of tertiary and vocational education, works with the National Education Commission (NEC) in drafting policy documents for TVET. As with general education, the NEC has developed a TVET policy (NEC 2018). The State Ministry of Skills Development, Vocational Education, Research & Innovation, which is mapped under the Ministry of Education, governs TVET. Nine TVET institutes are mapped under the state ministry, and other TVET institutes are embedded within 24 other national and state ministries. The state provides 73 percent of TVET, and private training institutes provide 27 percent.

Female TVET enrollment and completion in state TVET institutions has varied over time and among provinces. Female TVET enrollment as a share of the total rose from 40 percent in 2016 to 49 percent in 2021 (table 2.6). In 2021, the highest share of female enrollment was in the northwestern province (57 percent); the lowest was in the western province (43 percent). Female TVET completion as a share of the total increased from 41 percent in 2016 to 46 percent in 2021. In 2021, the highest female completion rate was in the northwestern province (62 percent); the lowest rates were in the northern and eastern provinces (both 36 percent).

COVID-19 affected TVET enrollment and completion rates. Between 2019 and 2021, TVET enrollments fell 32 percent (20 percent for women). The largest drop in enrollments occurred in the north-central province (49 percent) and the smallest in the Sabaragamuwa province (12 percent). Over the same period, completion rates fell 53 percent (51 percent for women). The sharpest reduction in the completion rate was in the north-central province (72 percent; 56 percent for women) and the lowest in the northern province (46 percent; 56 percent for women).

TABLE 2.6 Female TVET enrollment and completion in Sri Lanka, by province, various years

PROVINCE	ENROLLMENT									COMPLETION								
	2016			2019			2021			2016			2019			2021		
	TOTAL (N)	FEMALE (n)	SHARE OF FEMALES (%)	TOTAL (N)	FEMALE (n)	SHARE OF FEMALES (%)	TOTAL (N)	FEMALE (n)	SHARE OF FEMALES (%)	TOTAL (N)	FEMALE (n)	FEMALE SHARE COMPLETED (%)	TOTAL (N)	FEMALE (n)	FEMALE SHARE COMPLETED (%)	TOTAL (N)	FEMALE (n)	FEMALE SHARE COMPLETED (%)
Central	15,588	7,370	47	18,496	8,610	47	12,765	6,846	54	10,122	4,689	46	12,428	6,164	50	5,432	3,039	56
Eastern	13,594	5,124	38	19,687	7,823	40	13,854	6,779	49	9,394	3,704	39	13,466	5,618	42	6,493	2,344	36
Northern	10,406	3,665	35	11,252	4,819	43	8,022	3,980	50	7,199	2,438	34	8,948	3,940	44	4,804	1,745	36
North-central	7,958	2,969	37	12,614	4,252	34	6,478	3,266	50	5,526	1,846	33	8,773	2,762	31	2,457	1,420	58
Northwestern	13,108	6,112	47	15,929	7,723	48	11,296	6,485	57	8,729	4,067	47	10,166	5,280	52	4,700	2,901	62
Sabaragamuwa	9,085	3,990	44	12,159	4,957	41	10,655	5,493	52	6,237	2,662	43	8,323	3,738	45	3,683	1,746	47
Southern	21,084	9,146	43	25,416	11,934	47	18,408	9,336	51	15,044	6,424	43	17,324	8,567	49	7,914	4,296	54
Uva	6,655	2,719	41	9,030	4,106	45	7,153	3,754	52	4,309	1,729	40	5,969	2,887	48	3,192	1,850	58
Western	42,564	15,204	36	58,729	22,306	38	35,194	15,213	43	25,236	9,669	38	40,324	15,911	39	20,254	7,683	38
Total	**140,042**	**56,299**	**40**	**183,312**	**76,530**	**42**	**123,825**	**61,152**	**49**	**91,796**	**37,228**	**41**	**125,721**	**54,867**	**44**	**58,929**	**27,024**	**46**

Sources: Tertiary and Vocational Education Commission 2016, 2019, 2021.
Note: TVET = technical and vocational education and training.

TABLE 2.7 Female TVET enrollment and completion in STEM and non-STEM fields in Sri Lanka, various years

STREAM	2016 ENROLLMENT			2019 ENROLLMENT			2021 ENROLLMENT			2016 COMPLETION			2019 COMPLETION			2021 COMPLETION		
	TOTAL (N)	FEMALE (n)	FEMALE (%)	TOTAL (N)	FEMALE (n)	FEMALE (%)	TOTAL (N)	FEMALE (n)	FEMALE (%)	TOTAL (N)	FEMALE (n)	FEMALE (%)	TOTAL (N)	FEMALE (n)	FEMALE (%)	TOTAL (N)	FEMALE (n)	FEMALE (%)
Non-STEM	60,194	34,397	57	99,165	50,040	50	50,091	27,528	55	36,742	22,859	62	73,497	37,127	51	28,548	16,737	59
STEM	79,848	21,902	27	151,525	57,744	38	94,828	44,936	47	55,054	14,369	26	102,583	41,196	40	44,255	17,467	39
Total	140,042	56,299	40	250,690	107,784	43	144,919	72,464	50	91,796	37,228	41	176,080	78,323	44	72,803	34,204	47

Sources: Tertiary and Vocational Education Commission 2016, 2019, 2021; World Bank calculations.

Note: STEM = science, technology, engineering, and mathematics; TVET = technical and vocational education and training.

Women are increasingly engaged in STEM-related TVET. Female enrollments in TVET involving STEM fields jumped 164 percent from 2016 to 2019 but decreased by 22 percent from 2019 to 2021 during the COVID-19 pandemic (table 2.7). Moreover, female completion shot up 54 percent between 2016 and 2019, but COVID-19 lowered female completion of TVET in STEM fields by 2 percent between 2019 and 2021. Male enrollment and completion are higher in STEM fields because TVET is mainly seen as a male-dominated study stream.

STEM-RELATED HIGHER EDUCATION

Sri Lanka's higher education system is also complex. The Ministry of Education is responsible for higher education planning, delivery, management, quality assurance, and coordination. In addition, the NEC has proposed policies for higher education (NEC 2019), with the University Grants Commission (UGC) responsible for planning, maintaining quality standards, and coordinating funding for state higher education institutions. As of December 2021, the UGC has directly supervised 15 public universities and 29 state postgraduate institutions. In addition, Sri Lanka has 24 nonstate higher education institutions.

STEM courses are those offered by faculties or departments of medicine, dental science, veterinary science, agriculture, engineering, architecture and quantity surveying, computer science, science (bioscience and physical science), paramedical studies, and indigenous medicine. The rest—offered by faculties or departments of arts, education, management and commerce, and law—are non-STEM courses.

The number of undergraduates enrolled in STEM and non-STEM courses varies among state universities. In 2019, of the 128,188 students enrolled in 15 state universities, 49 percent (22 percent male and 27 percent female) took STEM courses and 51 percent took non-STEM courses (figure 2.5). The University of Moratuwa offered the most STEM courses, with 63 percent of men and 34 percent of women enrolled in engineering, architecture, and quantity surveying courses. At Uva Wellassa University, 34 percent of men and 48 percent of women were enrolled in STEM courses. The University of Visual and Performing Arts did not offer any STEM courses. At Eastern University, only 12 percent of male and 18 percent of female students were enrolled in STEM courses.

The number of graduates from state universities has varied over the years. Between 2011 and 2021, that number rose 12 percent (figure 2.6). Graduates in STEM subjects increased 39 percent, while those in non-STEM subjects fell 0.3 percent. STEM graduates accounted for 31 percent of the total in 2011 and 39 percent in 2021—the highest shares ever.

More female undergraduates in state universities are taking STEM courses. Between 2015 and 2021, the share of women earning an undergraduate degree in all fields increased from 68 to 70 percent (figure 2.7). During the same period, however, the share finishing STEM courses rose from 48 to 56 percent. More male students complete courses in engineering, architecture, quantity surveying, and computer science—while more female students finish courses in medicine, dental science, veterinary science, science, agriculture, paramedical science, and indigenous medicine. Paramedical studies have been the most popular STEM stream for women, with the share of female students rising from 69 percent in 2015 to 82 percent in 2021. The share of females in engineering

FIGURE 2.5

Enrollment in STEM and non-STEM courses in Sri Lanka, by university and gender, 2019

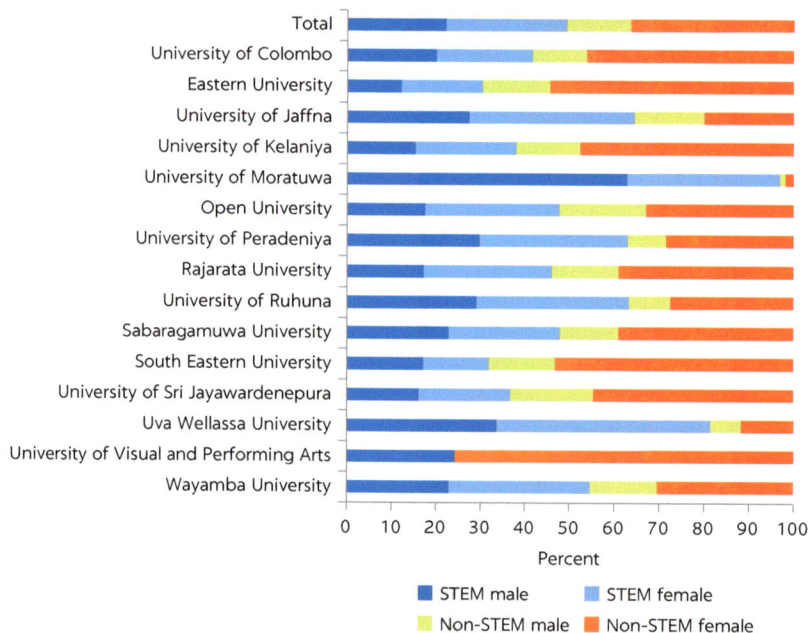

Source: University Grants Commission 2019.
Note: STEM = science, technology, engineering, and mathematics.

FIGURE 2.6

STEM and non-STEM graduates of state universities in Sri Lanka, 2011–21

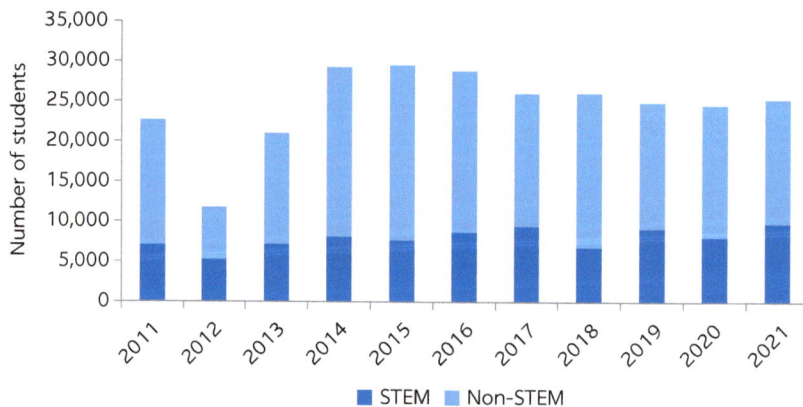

Sources: University Grants Commission, 2011–21; World Bank calculations.
Note: STEM = science, technology, engineering, and mathematics.

increased from 22 percent in 2015 to 30 percent in 2021, while the share in architecture and quantity surveying courses plummeted from 73 percent to 44 percent. Between 2015 and 2021, about 75 percent of females finished non-STEM courses (arts, education, management and commerce, and law), with the largest share in education.

Nonstate higher education institutions contribute to undergraduate STEM output. In 2021, the ministry in charge of higher education recognized 24 nonstate higher education institutions offering 190 degree programs. Most nonstate

FIGURE 2.7

Females completing STEM and non-STEM courses in state universities in Sri Lanka, various years

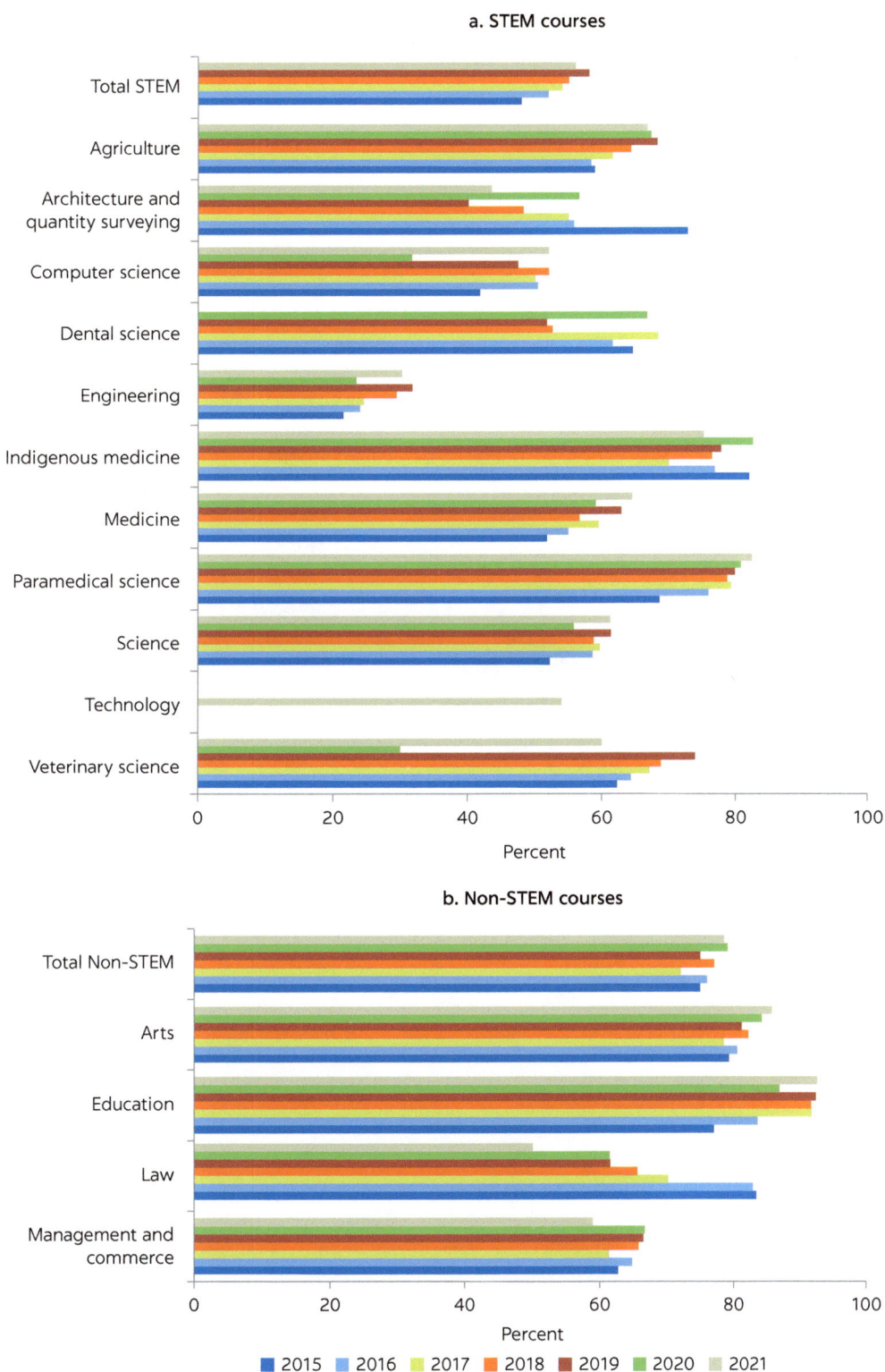

Sources: University Grants Commission 2015, 2016, 2017, 2018, 2019, 2020, 2021.
Note: STEM = science, technology, engineering, and mathematics.

TABLE 2.8 **STEM and non-STEM female postgraduate degrees in Sri Lanka, 2015, 2019, and 2021**

STREAM	2015			2019			2021		
	TOTAL (N)	FEMALES (n)	FEMALES (%)	TOTAL (N)	FEMALES (n)	FEMALES (%)	TOTAL (N)	FEMALES (n)	FEMALES (%)
STEM	2,049	842	41	2,858	1,325	46	2,420	1,253	52
Non-STEM	5,464	2,870	53	7,133	4,315	60	7,702	4,887	63
Total	**7,513**	**3,712**	**49**	**9,991**	**5,640**	**56**	**10,122**	**6,140**	**61**

Sources: University Grants Commission 2015, 2019, 2021.
Note: STEM = science, technology, engineering, and mathematics.

higher education institutions focus on ICT, health science, and other popular science-related courses. In 2018, more than 58 percent of students in nonstate higher education institutions took STEM-related courses (Ministry of Higher Education, Technology and Innovations 2019). In addition to nonstate higher education institutions, professional bodies affiliated with foreign countries—such as the British Computer Society and Australian Computer Society—offer degree courses.

More female postgraduate students earn non-STEM than STEM degrees. Between 2015 and 2021, the number of students receiving postgraduate degrees increased 35 percent for all fields and 18 percent for STEM subject areas (table 2.8). The number of women earning postgraduate degrees increased 65 percent for all fields and 49 percent for STEM subjects. In addition, women accounted for 41 percent of postgraduate STEM degrees in 2015, 46 percent in 2019, and 52 percent in 2021. Postgraduate enrollment in STEM fields should be encouraged further.

In 2021, science and information technology (IT) streams accounted for the most postgraduate degrees in STEM, followed by medicine, dental, and allied health science. The largest shares of female postgraduate degrees in STEM were in veterinary science (86 percent), agriculture (71 percent), architecture (59 percent), and medicine, dental, and allied health science (58 percent). The highest number of female postgraduate degrees in STEM was in science/IT, followed by medicine, dental, and allied health science (figure 2.8). Education accounted for the largest share of non-STEM postgraduate degrees (73 percent females), with some teachers who received postgraduate qualifications in education likely to teach STEM subjects.

STEM LABOR MARKET LANDSCAPE

In 2019, the labor force in Sri Lanka consisted of 8.1 million workers, only 34 percent of whom were female (table 2.9). Around 45 percent of workers were engaged in STEM-related occupations. Men accounted for 30 percent and women for 15 percent of the labor force in STEM-related occupations. The number of women in STEM-related occupations increased 11 percent between 2015 and 2019.

After TVET, men are far more likely than women to be placed in jobs—regardless of qualifications, province, or sector. The differences are stark, with TVET job placement occurring for

- 61 percent of men and 37 percent of women lacking National Vocational Qualification (NVQ) certificates,

FIGURE 2.8

STEM and non-STEM postgraduate degrees in Sri Lanka, by stream, 2021

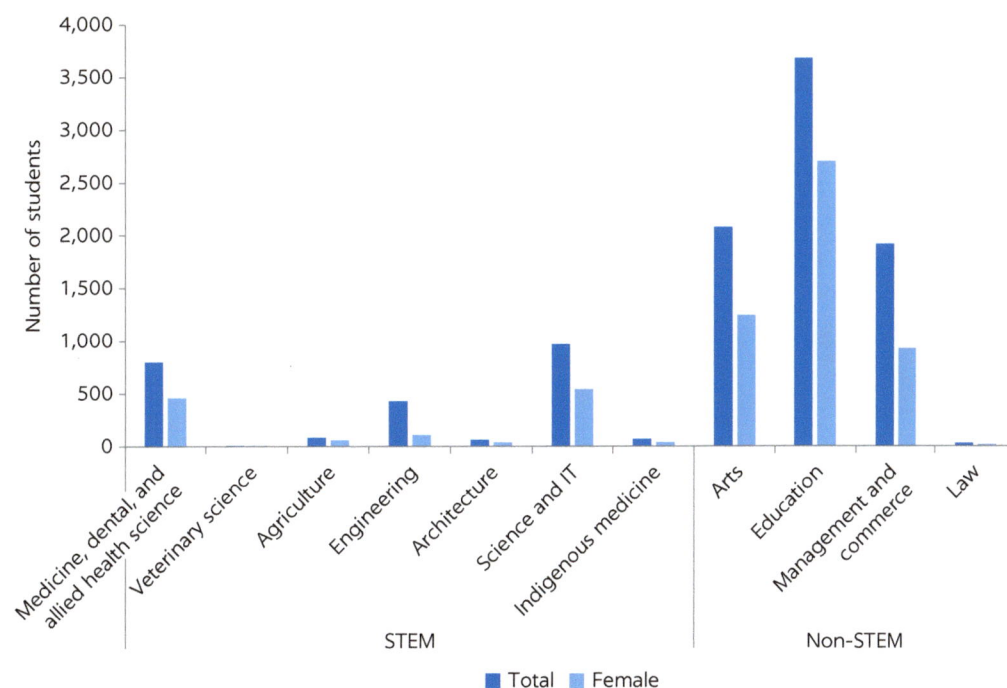

Source: University Grants Commission 2021.
Note: IT = information technology; STEM = science, technology, engineering, and mathematics.

TABLE 2.9 **Employment in Sri Lanka by occupational group and gender, 2015–19**

YEAR	TOTAL			STEM OCCUPATIONS			
	TOTAL (*N*)	MALE (*n*)	FEMALE (*n*)	MALE (*n*)	MALE (%)	FEMALE (*n*)	FEMALE (%)
2015	7,830,976	5,097,797	2,733,179	2,212,511	28	1,120,151	14
2016	7,947,683	5,149,948	2,797,735	2,289,462	29	1,168,439	15
2017	8,208,179	5,279,158	2,929,021	2,497,399	30	1,283,643	16
2018	8,015,165	5,300,310	2,714,855	2,512,682	31	1,152,363	14
2019	8,180,692	5,368,896	2,811,796	2,477,706	30	1,239,141	15

Sources: Department of Census & Statistics 2019; World Bank calculations.
Note: STEM = science, technology, engineering, and mathematics.

- 66 percent of men and 40 percent of women with NVQ certificates, and
- 84 percent of men and 78 percent of women with NVQ degrees (Asian Development Bank 2018).

The TVET female job placement rate was highest in the western province (51 percent) and lowest in the eastern province (21 percent; figure 2.9). By sector, TVET female job placement was highest in construction (55 percent) and nonexistent in hotel and tourism and in metal and light engineering.

Graduates of state higher education institutions are more likely to be employed if they hold STEM degrees. In 2016–17, all graduates with degrees in computer science/IT and architecture degrees were employed, followed by 96 percent for allied health science, 92 percent for engineering, and 83 percent

FIGURE 2.9

TVET job placement rates in Sri Lanka, by gender, province, and sector, 2016

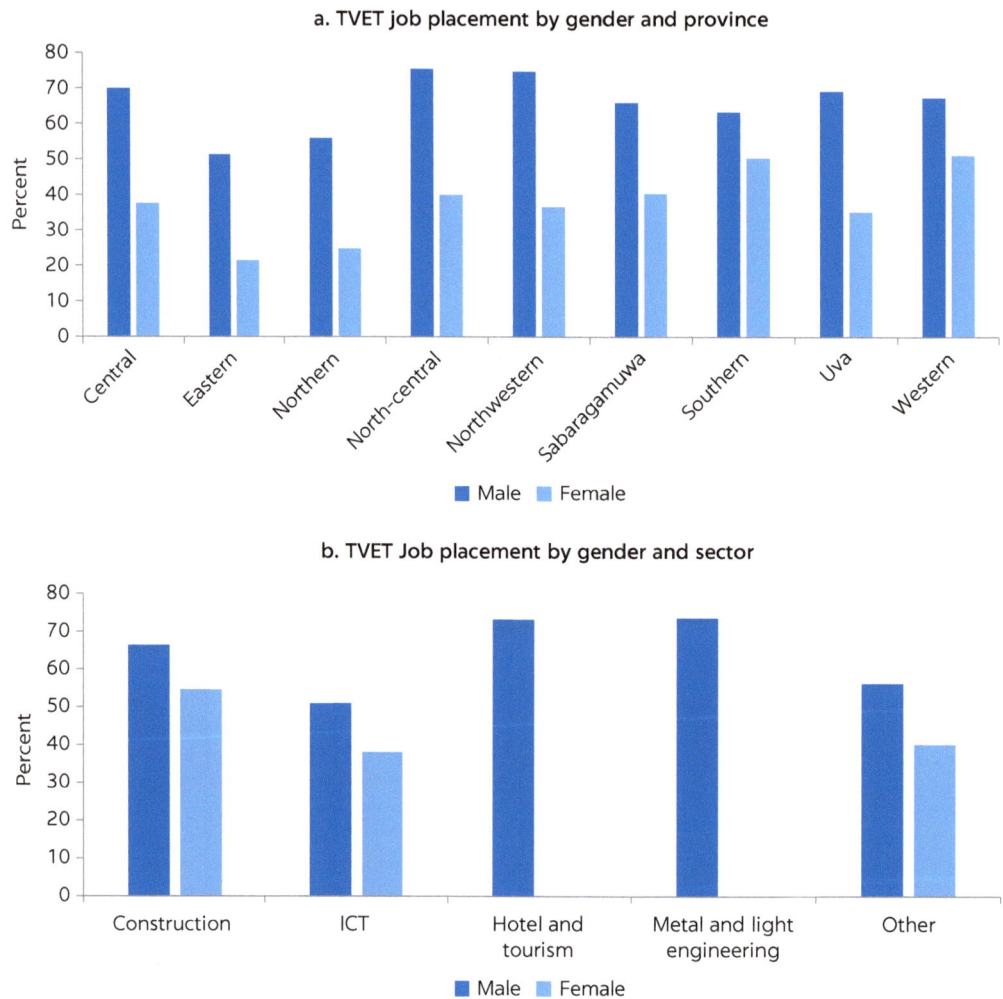

a. TVET job placement by gender and province

Male   Female

b. TVET Job placement by gender and sector

Male   Female

Source: Asian Development Bank 2018.
Note: TVET female job placement was nonexistent in hotel and tourism and in metal and light engineering.

for both science and agriculture (figure 2.10). Among graduates with non-STEM degrees, employment rates were highest in education (100 percent), law (86 percent), and management (72 percent)—and lowest in the performing arts (37 percent).

Graduates with STEM degrees also find their first jobs much faster. In state higher education institutions, 82 percent of computer science/IT students, 63 percent of engineering students, and 60 percent of architecture students find their first jobs during school or after taking their final examination (figure 2.11). In non-STEM fields, only 55 percent of management students and 50 percent of law students do so, and although there is full employment for those with education degrees, it takes 7–12 months for most to find their first jobs.

ICT graduates work in four types of organizations. Business process management firms have the highest share of female employees with ICT degrees (49 percent), followed by public entities (40 percent), non-ICT companies (36 percent), and ICT companies (29 percent).

FIGURE 2.10

Employment status of STEM and non-STEM graduates of state higher education institutions in Sri Lanka, 2016–17

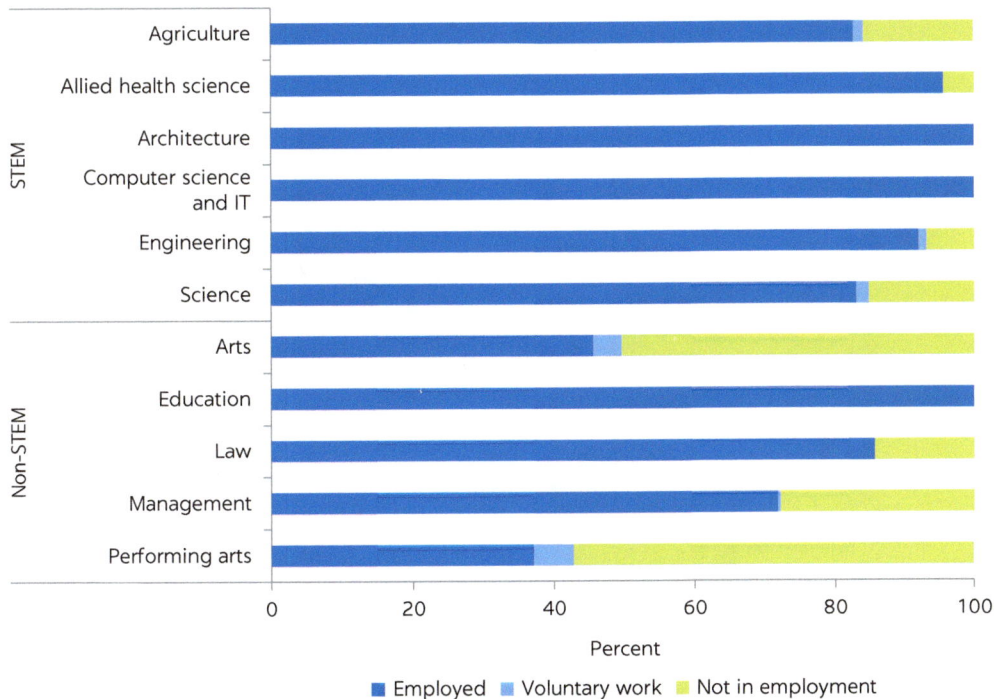

Source: University Grants Commission 2018.
Note: IT = information technology; STEM = science, technology, engineering, and mathematics.

FIGURE 2.11

Time taken to get first job for STEM and non-STEM graduates of state higher education institutions in Sri Lanka, 2018

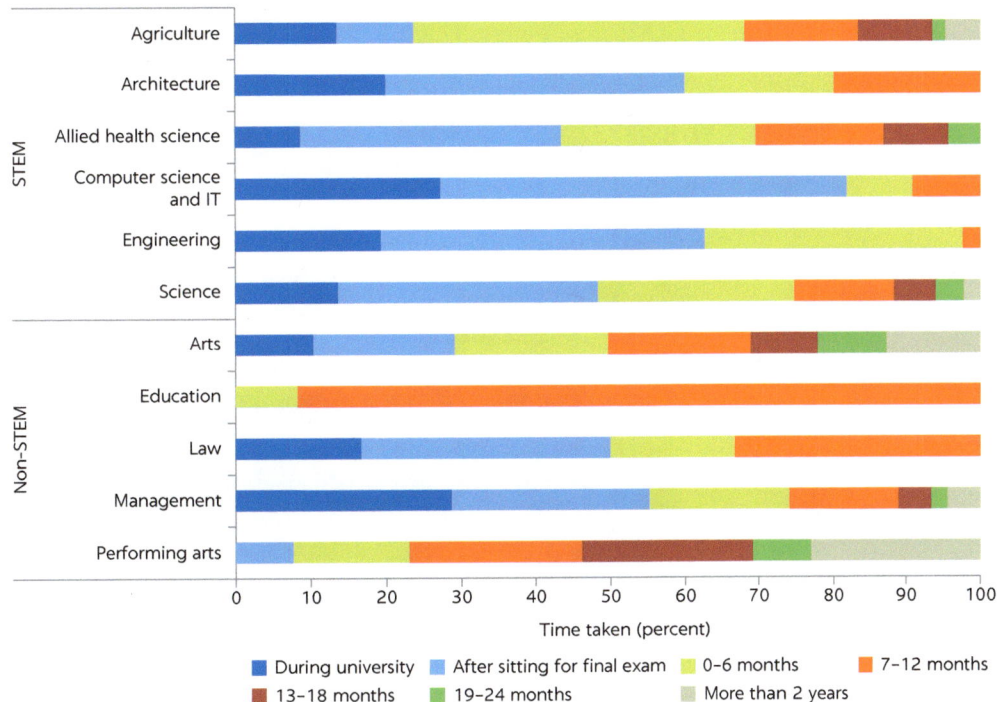

Source: University Grants Commission 2018b.
Note: IT = information technology; STEM = science, technology, engineering, and mathematics.

ICT workers have a range of qualifications. Of the 64 percent with an ICT bachelor's degree, 19 percent are women and 45 percent are men (figure 2.12). In addition, 4 percent of female and 7 percent of male ICT workers have non-ICT degrees. Twelve percent of ICT workers have a diploma or higher diploma, while 4 percent lack formal qualifications.

FIGURE 2.12

Qualifications of information and communications technology workers in Sri Lanka, by gender, 2019

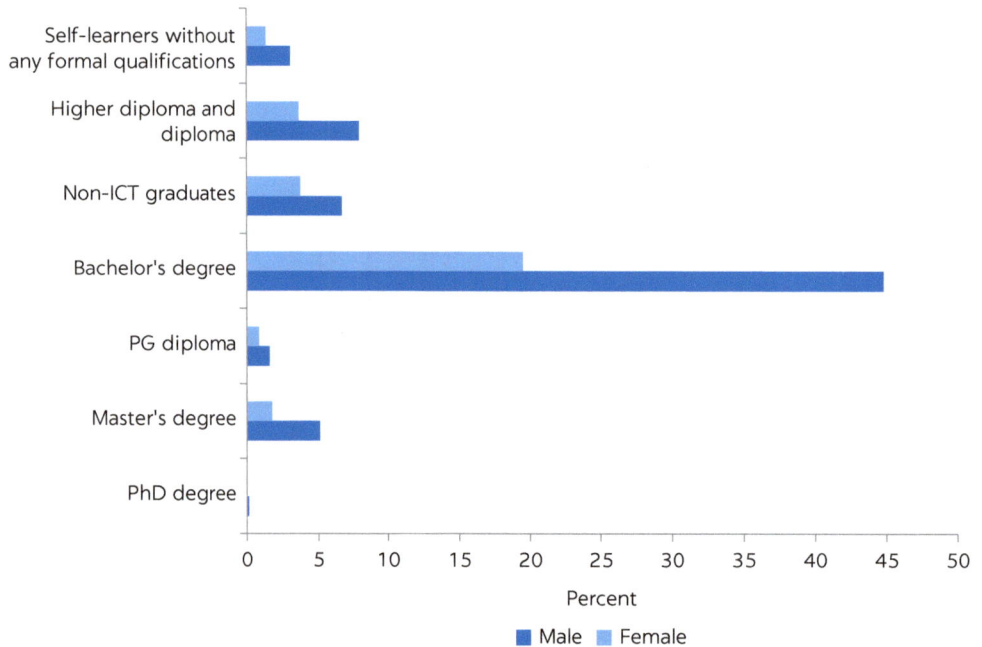

Sources: Information Communication Technology Agency 2019; original calculations for this publication.
Note: IT = information technology; PG = postgraduate; PhD = Doctor of Philosophy.

FIGURE 2.13

Composition of the information and communications technology workforce in Sri Lanka, by years of experience and gender, 2018

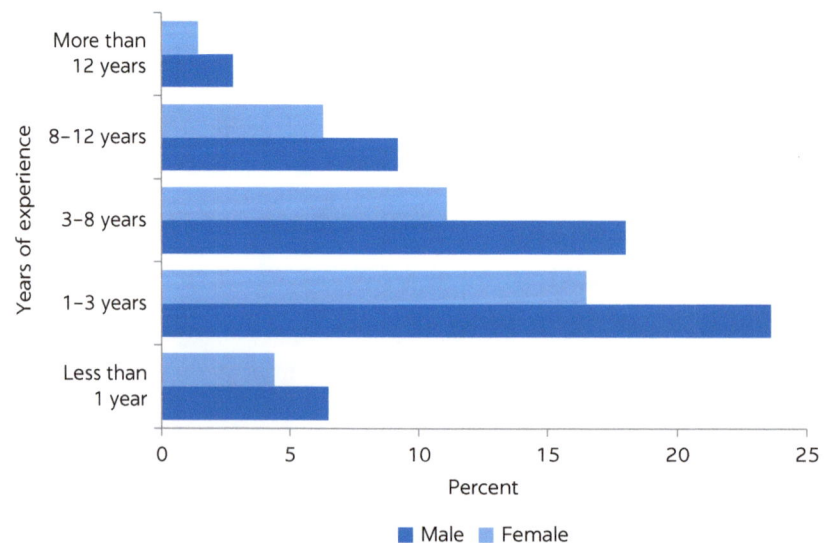

Source: Information Communication Technology Agency 2019.

The ICT workforce tends to have limited experience, with the number of years of work experience being an indicator of the quality of a workforce. Very few female ICT workers (1 percent) have more than 12 years of work experience (figure 2.13). Nearly 20 percent of ICT workers have more than 8 years of work experience (12 percent of men and 8 percent of women). More than half of ICT workers have less than 3 years of experience (21 percent of women and 30 percent of men). Most female ICT workers have 1–3 years (17 percent) or 3–8 years (11 percent) of work experience. These data indicate that much of the ICT workforce consists of young female workers—which is also a sign that only in recent years have girls become interested in pursuing ICT degrees.

REFERENCES

Anjum, S. 2015. "Gender Difference in Mathematics Achievement and Its Relation with Reading Comprehension of Children at Upper Primary Stage." *Journal of Education and Practice* 6 (16): 71–5.

Asian Development Bank. 2018. *Tracer Study: Sri Lanka: Public Training Institutions in 2016.* Manila: Asian Development Bank. http://dx.doi.org/10.22617/TCS189781-2.

Aturupane, Harsha, Hideki Higashi, Roshini Ebenezer, Deepika Attygalle, Shobhana Sosale, Sangeeta Dey, and Rehana Wijesinghe. 2021. *Sri Lanka Human Capital Development: Realizing the Promise and Potential of Human Capital.* International Development in Focus. Washington, DC: World Bank. https://openknowledge.worldbank.org /handle/10986/36113 License: CC BY 3.0 IGO.

Department of Census & Statistics. 2019. "Labour Force Survey: Annual Report." Colombo.

Department of Examination. 2014. "Performance of Candidates General Certificate Examination Advanced Level." Colombo.

Department of Examination. 2015a. "Performance of Candidates General Certificate Examination Advanced Level." Colombo.

Department of Examination. 2015b. "Performance of Candidates General Certificate Examination Ordinary Level." Colombo.

Department of Examination. 2016. "Performance of Candidates General Certificate Examination Advanced Level." Colombo.

Department of Examination. 2017. "Performance of Candidates General Certificate Examination Advanced Level." Colombo.

Department of Examination. 2018. "Performance of Candidates General Certificate Examination Advanced Level." Colombo.

Department of Examination. 2019. "Performance of Candidates General Certificate Examination Advanced Level." Colombo.

Department of Examination. 2020. "Performance of Candidates General Certificate Examination Advanced Level." Colombo.

Department of Examination. 2021. "Performance of Candidates Grade 5 Scholarship Examination." Colombo.

Information Communication Technology Agency. 2019. "National IT-BPM Workforce Survey 2019." Colombo.

Ministry of Education. 2018. "Annual School Census." Colombo.

Ministry of Education. 2019. "Annual School Census." Colombo.

Ministry of Education. 2020. "Annual School Census." Colombo.

Ministry of Higher Education, Technology and Innovations. 2019. "Higher Education: Annual Report." Colombo.

National Education Commission. 2018. "National Policy on Technical & Vocational Education." Colombo.

National Education Commission. 2019. "National Policy Proposals on Higher Education." Colombo.

National Education Research and Evaluation Centre. 2003. "National Report: National Assessment of Achievement of Students Completing Grade 4 in Year 2002 in Sri Lanka." Colombo.

National Education Research and Evaluation Centre. 2004. "National Report: National Assessment of Achievement of Students Completing Grade 4 in Year 2002 in Sri Lanka." Colombo.

National Education Research and Evaluation Centre. 2013. "National Report: National Assessment of Achievement of Students Completing Grade 8 in Year 2012 in Sri Lanka." Colombo.

National Education Research and Evaluation Centre. 2015. "National Report: National Assessment of Achievement of Students Completing Grade 8 in Year 2014 in Sri Lanka." Colombo.

National Education Research and Evaluation Centre. 2017. "National Report: National Assessment of Achievement of Students Completing Grade 8 in Year 2016 in Sri Lanka." Colombo.

Tertiary and Vocational Education Commission. 2016. "Labour Market Information Bulletin." Colombo.

Tertiary and Vocational Education Commission. 2019. "Labour Market Information Bulletin." Colombo.

Tertiary and Vocational Education Commission. 2021. "Labour Market Information Bulletin." Colombo.

University Grants Commission. 2011. "Annual Report." Colombo.

University Grants Commission. 2012. "Annual Report." Colombo.

University Grants Commission. 2013. "Annual Report." Colombo.

University Grants Commission. 2014. "Annual Report." Colombo.

University Grants Commission. 2015. "Annual Report." Colombo.

University Grants Commission. 2016. "Annual Report." Colombo.

University Grants Commission. 2017. "Annual Report." Colombo.

University Grants Commission. 2018a. "Annual Report." Colombo.

University Grants Commission. 2018b. "Tracer Study of Graduate Universities in Sri Lanka." Colombo.

University Grants Commission. 2019. "Annual Report." Colombo.

University Grants Commission. 2020. "Annual Report." Colombo.

University Grants Commission. 2021. "Annual Report." Colombo.

3 Factors Enabling or Preventing Access to STEM for Women

ANALYZING THE EVIDENCE

Numerous factors enable and prevent women's access to science, technology, engineering, and mathematics (STEM) education and careers in Sri Lanka. These include macroeconomic conditions; the country's poverty profile; policy, governance, quality, and financial issues for school education, technical and vocational education and training (TVET), higher education, and labor market participation; and sociocultural factors.

MACROECONOMIC FACTORS

In 2018, Sri Lanka was classified as an upper-middle-income country, with gross domestic product (GDP) per capita of $4,102. In 2019, when economic growth slowed, it was downgraded to a lower-middle-income country with GDP per capita of $3,852. In May 2022, Sri Lanka began experiencing an economic crisis, with the economy expecting to contract in 2022 (by –9.2 percent) and 2023 (–4.2 percent) as foreign exchange shortages continue and job and income losses intensify (World Bank 2022). Slower economic growth could create opportunities in some sectors and hinder growth in others.

POVERTY PROFILE

During the 2010s, poverty in Sri Lanka fell dramatically, from 6.7 percent of the population (1.3 million people) in 2012–13 to 4.1 percent (843,913) in 2016 (Department of Census & Statistics [DCS] 2017b). Social protection measures helped reduce poverty, while social assistance efforts—such as scholarships and school meal programs—boosted school attendance and learning outcomes. Poverty increased, however, due to the COVID-19 lockdown and job losses, and it was expected to double to more than 25 percent between 2021 and 2022 (World Bank 2022).

SCHOOL FACTORS

Several policies have enhanced access to education, starting with the introduction of free public school education in 1947. The provision of free textbooks and subsidized transport further boosted access, and students in less developed areas now receive free footwear and school meals. In addition, the government introduced 13 years of guaranteed education by adding a vocational stream for students who do not complete the General Certificate of Education (GCE) for the Ordinary Level (O/L).

The governance structure and type of school enable or prevent access to STEM education. Children attending type 1AB schools can study science at the collegiate level. Children in type 1C schools cannot, and only a few type 1C schools offer technology options at the collegiate level. Students who attend type 2 and 3 schools can apply to type 1AB or type 1C schools after grade 8 or 11.

The quality of subject streams varies for the GCE Advanced Level (A/L). The student/teacher ratio for GCE A/L classes indicates a shortage of teachers in some schools for a few subject streams. The average student/teacher ratio for GCE A/L subject streams is 12.8, which is excellent, but the ratio for "other subject" streams (0.09) has lowered the average. The "other subject" stream is not offered in every school, and fewer students pursue it. The student/teacher ratio for the technology stream is the highest, at 35.3, indicating severe shortages of technology teachers.

Teachers with professional qualifications enhance student learning. In 2018, around 45 percent of teachers held a degree, a 28 percent increase from 2012 (table 3.1). The number of graduate teachers with professional qualifications increased 43 percent during that time. The number of graduate teachers without professional qualifications rose 5 percent. In 2018, some 97 percent of teachers were graduates or trained.

The Ministry of Education has developed a manual on career guidance to help education officers, principals, and teachers present students with subject and career options. In 2020, the manual was shared online with students who sat for the GCE A/L. Career guidance programs offered in grade 9 help students select subjects such as information and communications technology (ICT), agriculture, and food technology as optional subjects in grades 10 and 11. In addition, career guidance programs offered during the senior secondary period can encourage students to select a science or technology stream for the GCE A/L.

Lab facilities are among the infrastructure needed to enhance STEM learning. Science labs are available in all type 1AB schools offering a science stream for

TABLE 3.1 **Qualifications of teachers in state schools in Sri Lanka, various years**

DESCRIPTION	2012	2015	2017	2018
Graduates	86,751	96,200	106,742	110,741
With professional qualifications	51,814	71,448	75,429	74,212
Without professional qualifications	34,937	27,556	31,313	36,529
Trained teachers	128,152	132,952	129,616	130,635
Unskilled/trainee/other	8,430	5,042	4,660	5,958
Total	**223,333**	**236,998**	**241,018**	**247,334**

Sources: Ministry of Education 2012, 2015, 2017b, 2018.

the GCE A/L. Many schools also need information technology labs. In 2017, only 72 percent of type 1AB and 1C schools and 19 percent of type 2 and 3 schools had such labs.

Materials are also needed to run experiments. Mathematics teaching for activity-based learning is needed at the primary and secondary levels. Although arrangements have been made to promote mathematics labs, some teachers dislike using technology (Polgampala, Shen, and Huang 2016). This fear could be alleviated by providing training and, in the future, designing classrooms and supplying equipment and software to encourage STEM education.

Curricula for mathematics, science, ICT, and technology subjects must be reviewed and revised to prepare students for the world of work in the twenty-first century. This has already happened for science and mathematics for grades 6, 7, 9, 10, 11, and 13. New electronic media textbooks have also been developed. Curriculum review and revision must be a continuous process because subject contents must include relevant information and exercises to impart fresh knowledge and skills to students.

Activities have been developed to popularize STEM subjects in schools. The Ministry of Education in Sri Lanka, together with partner organizations, has coordinated several national-level competitions in science, mathematics, information technology, agriculture, and other subjects to encourage students to participate in national and international competitions. In addition, school-based societies have been formed to conduct activities such as exhibitions, develop newsletters, and the like. In addition, the Ministry of Science, Technology, and Research and the Sri Lanka Advancement of Science have organized workshops to inculcate science, technology, and research in schools and to train teachers at the national and provincial levels. National programs to set up model laboratories for training of trainer programs have been organized for master science teachers, science teacher instructors, and zonal assistant directors of science.

School education has improved over time, but more investments are needed to achieve better outcomes. Per capita student spending increased 44 percent between 2014 and 2017 (table 3.2). In 2017, the Ministry of Education accounted for 27 percent and Provincial Councils for 73 percent of total spending. Recurrent spending and capital spending accounted for 78 percent and 22 percent of the total, respectively. It is imperative to increase capital spending to provide more labs for science and mathematics and computer rooms with modern equipment to encourage more students to learn science, mathematics, and ICT.

Foreign financing agencies encourage STEM in school education. The World Bank's General Education Modernization Project provides financing to improve mathematics learning outcomes, develop digitally enabled books in mathematics, and increase the number of new professionally qualified teachers (World Bank 2018). Vacant positions in schools will be filled by professionally qualified teachers; at least half should be women. Their professional qualifications can be improved by attending school-based training on pedagogical skills, motivation, and classroom management and registering in master's programs to enhance technical knowledge among teacher educators, curriculum developers, and education administrators. The Asian Development Bank's School Sector Development Program helped introduce the technology stream in 251 schools, meet gender targets in recruiting

TABLE 3.2 Capital spending in school education in Sri Lanka, various years

Millions of Sri Lanka Rupees

	2014		2015		2017	
DESCRIPTION	COST	%	COST	%	COST	%
Ministry of Education (MoE)						
Capital	15,789	9	15,536	8	27,711	9
Recurrent	36,592	22	38,896	19	52,057	18
Total	**52,381**	**31**	**54,432**	**26**	**79,768**	**27**
Provincial Councils (PCs)						
Capital	20,000	12	24,130	12	36,922	13
Recurrent	97,000	57	127,000	62	176,197	60
Total	**117,000**	**69**	**151,130**	**74**	**213,119**	**73**
Total (MoE and PCs)						
Capital	35,789	21	39,666	19	64,633	22
Recurrent	133,592	79	165,896	81	228,254	78
Total	**169,381**	**100**	**205,562**	**100**	**292,887**	**100**

Source: Sri Lanka Ministry of Education 2017a.

technology stream teachers, and increase the percentage of female students in science (Asian Development Bank 2020a). In addition, the Asian Development Bank's Secondary Education Sector Program has been designed to strengthen STEM education by increasing the number of type 1AB schools, supplying necessary equipment, training teachers, developing curricula to impart twenty-first-century skills, and conducting gender-sensitive national media campaigns (Asian Development Bank 2020b).

TVET FACTORS

Several TVET policies promote participation. The free TVET Policy, introduced in 2017, increased the number of students enrolled in TVET courses. To encourage female participation, in 2017, the ministry in charge of skills development prepared a Gender Equality and Social Inclusion Framework that helped Skills Sector Councils find potential jobs for women in nontraditional sectors. Based on those initiatives, organizations have prepared competency standards to conduct training. In addition, the Women's Advisory Committee has been set up to encourage women to act as role models and promote female participation in TVET.

The 2021 budget for the government of Sri Lanka included an LKR 4,000 bursary for full-time TVET students. Programs covered include apprenticeships and on-the-job programs to encourage industry participation. The TVET entrepreneurship development training program allows women to obtain loans from the Self-Employment Promotion Initiative scheme.

Skills remain fragmented, and training providers are listed under many ministries. Thus, coordination and administration issues need to be addressed to get all trainees accurately assessed to receive National Vocational Qualification certificates. The One TVET initiative has been proposed to unify the fragmented system.

Female enrollment is extremely low in some courses due to the perception that some occupations and trades are more masculine. In 2019, courses with an incredibly small number of female students registered included the National Certificate in Engineering (Motor Vehicle Mechanic), Craft Level (Automobile Mechanic; one female student), and National Certificate (Motorcycle Mechanic; five female students). The National Certificate in Welding had no females registered. The Ceylon German Technical Training Institute had five female students registered in 2019 (Tertiary and Vocational Education Commission 2019). Discussions with female students indicate that some register for predominantly male training courses, such as construction, with the goal of becoming teachers.

There is a severe shortage of qualified TVET teachers. The vacancy rate of teaching staff varied among training institutes that came under the State Ministry of Skills Development, Vocational Education, Research & Innovation (SMSDVERI). The overall teaching staff vacancy rate fell from 39 percent in 2015 to 35 percent in 2019 (table 3.3). The highest teacher vacancy rate (50 percent) was in the Department of Technical Education & Training, and the lowest (7 percent) was at the University of Vocational Technology. Although the number of students enrolled in TVET increased, teaching positions did not keep pace. Accordingly, the student/teacher ratio rose from 39.68 to 48.44 between 2015 and 2019. That ratio varied among training institutes, with the highest student/teacher ratio at the National Youth Services Council. TVET teaching staff has been dominated by men (66 percent), and the Ceylon German Technical Training Institute has only around 2 percent female staff, but teacher qualifications and training have increased in recent years. Between 2015 and 2019, 636 teaching staff received a National Vocational Qualification level 5 certificate in technical teacher education, and 2,702 teachers underwent industry exposure training programs. Further improvements are needed, however, to enhance the quality of teachers. A lack of career development opportunities and low remuneration levels have impeded the recruitment of qualified teachers.

There is a disconnect between curricula and industry requirements. Continuous improvements in curricula will help students acquire the

TABLE 3.3 **Teaching staff at selected TVET institutes in Sri Lanka, 2015 and 2019**

INSTITUTE	NUMBER OF TEACHING STAFF (EXCLUDING VISITING STAFF)		TEACHING STAFF VACANCY RATE (%)		FEMALE STAFF (%)	STUDENT TO TEACHER RATIO	
	2015	2019	2015	2019	2019	2015	2019
CGTTI	150	153	4	10	2	26.83	7.64
DTET	535	670	60	50	27	37.13	63.67
NAITA	395	441	46	39	46	57.10	68.00
NYSC	85	134	47	17	34	222.98	166.27
OCUSL	30	69	21	15	39	30.60	1.68
UNIVOTEC	39	52	28	7	52	20.49	20.00
VTA	1,182	1,272	20	26	37	24.32	29.82
Total	**2,416**	**2,791**	**39**	**35**	**34**	**39.68**	**48.44**

Sources: Tertiary and Vocational Education Commission 2019; administrative data from the Skills Sector Development Division; World Bank calculations.
Note: CGTTI = Ceylon German Technical Training Institute; DTET = Department of Technical Education & Training; NAITA = National Apprentice Industrial Training Authority; NYSC = National Youth Services Council; OCUSL = Ocean University of Sri Lanka; UNIVOTEC = University of Vocational Technology; VTA = Vocational Training Authority.

competencies required by the world of work. Input from the Skills Council and the National Apprentice Industrial Training Authority is needed to improve curricula and make them gender sensitive. A curriculum review must include STEM-oriented competencies and activities to prepare students for the workforce (International Labour Organization 2021).

Further investments in TVET are needed to prepare young people to join the labor market. SMSDVERI spending on skills development as a share of the total rose from 32 percent in 2017 to 36 percent in 2021 (table 3.4). Capital spending decreased from 2017 to 2021. TVET has attracted financing from multilateral and other foreign agencies, with the share of foreign financing tripling from 4 percent in 2017 to 13 percent in 2019, but decreasing to only 2 percent in 2022 due to the economic crisis in Sri Lanka.

HIGHER EDUCATION FACTORS

Several policies enhance and encourage access to higher education. University admissions are based on merit. The University Grants Commission determines the cutoff marks for each province. State higher education institutes offer courses free of charge; students pay only a nominal registration fee. Students also pay a nominal fee for hostel facilities, with women's hostels located within or close to universities. In 2018, 84 hostels housed 33,600 students (Ministry of Higher Education 2018), and several other hostels were being built. Cafeterias in universities offer affordable food. Several welfare programs are provided to encourage students to register and complete courses. In addition, most universities have developed subject and stream policies that include internships in the third or final year of degree programs.

The government has obtained foreign funding to enhance access to STEM-related subjects in higher education. The World Bank's Accelerating Higher Education Expansion and Development Operation's first two project goals focus on increasing the STEM enrollments in higher education institutes (World Bank 2017). The third focuses on encouraging research, development, and innovation. This goal will be achieved by offering competitive, performance-based research grants; developing performance-based research and innovation commercialization programs; and supporting programs linking universities and businesses to increase collaboration and technology transfer. In addition, academic staff will receive scholarships to pursue higher education.

The policy on expanding access to STEM education will be achieved by creating new university departments and expanding faculties for STEM courses. The government has already constructed buildings for new university departments and faculties. New faculties of medicine will be set up at the universities of Moratuwa, Sabaragamuwa, and Wayamba, along with health sciences faculties at Eastern University.

More academic staff are working in STEM-related subject streams. Between 2015 and 2021, the number of academic staff working in STEM fields rose from 3,084 to 4,369—a 42 percent increase (table 3.5). The total number of academic staff increased by 35 percent during the same period, and the number of non-STEM academic staff jumped by 25 percent. The number of STEM professors increased 74 percent, senior lecturers 32 percent, and lecturers 43 percent.

The highest numbers of STEM professors and senior lecturers are in the science, medicine, engineering, and agriculture fields, and those in arts and humanities and management studies work in non-STEM fields (figure 3.1).

TABLE 3.4 Spending on skills development and vocational education in Sri Lanka, 2017–21

Thousands of Sri Lanka Rupees

TYPE OF SPENDING	2017	2018	2019	2020 REVISED	2021 REVISED	2022 ESTIMATED	2023 FORECASTED	TREND
Operational								
Recurrent	3,658,453	4,531,738	4,632,770	4,526,045	5,264,300	5,410,100	5,583,760	
Capital	531,392	1,198,370	990,550	10,043	100,000	30,000	30,930	
Subtotal	4,189,845	5,730,108	5,623,320	4,536,088	5,364,300	5,440,100	5,614,690	
Development								
Recurrent	243,134	80,000	77,000	56,671	560,000	1,000,000	1,000,000	
Capital	1,735,243	3,199,202	3,298,000	2,114,249	2,419,500	2,720,000	743,000	
Subtotal	1,978,377	3,279,202	3,375,000	2,170,920	2,979,500	3,720,000	1,743,000	
Total	**6,168,222**	**9,009,310**	**8,998,320**	**6,707,008**	**8,343,800**	**9,160,100**	**7,357,690**	
% Operational	68%	64%	62%	68%	64%	59%	76%	
% Development	32%	36%	38%	32%	36%	41%	24%	
Financing								
Foreign financed	219,650	996,202	1,169,000	1,121,147	511,900	180,000	590,000	
% Foreign funding	4%	11%	13%	17%	6%	2%	8%	

Source: World Bank calculations based on Ministry of Finance budget estimates. This excludes expenditures incurred for the Department of Technical Education & Training.
Note: The skills development and vocational training program budget was under the Ministry of Finance and Ministry of National Policies, Economic Affairs, Resettlement and Rehabilitation, Northern Province Development, Vocational Training and Skills Development and Youth Affairs in 2020.

TABLE 3.5 University academic staff in Sri Lanka, by STEM and non-STEM streams 2015 and 2021

STREAM	2015				2021				GROWTH 2015 TO 2021 (%)			
	PROFESSORS	SENIOR LECTURERS	LECTURERS	TOTAL	PROFESSORS	SENIOR LECTURERS	LECTURERS	TOTAL	PROFESSORS	SENIOR LECTURERS	LECTURERS	TOTAL
STEM	460	1,589	1,035	3,084	802	2,092	1,475	4,369	74	32	43	42
Non-STEM	227	1,167	721	2,115	383	1,439	813	2,635	69	23	13	25
Total	**687**	**2,756**	**1,756**	**5,199**	**1,185**	**3,531**	**2,288**	**7,004**	**72**	**28**	**30**	**35**

Sources: University Grants Commission 2015, 2021.
Note: STEM = science, technology, engineering, and mathematics.

FIGURE 3.1

Academic staff by STEM and non-STEM stream in Sri Lanka, 2021

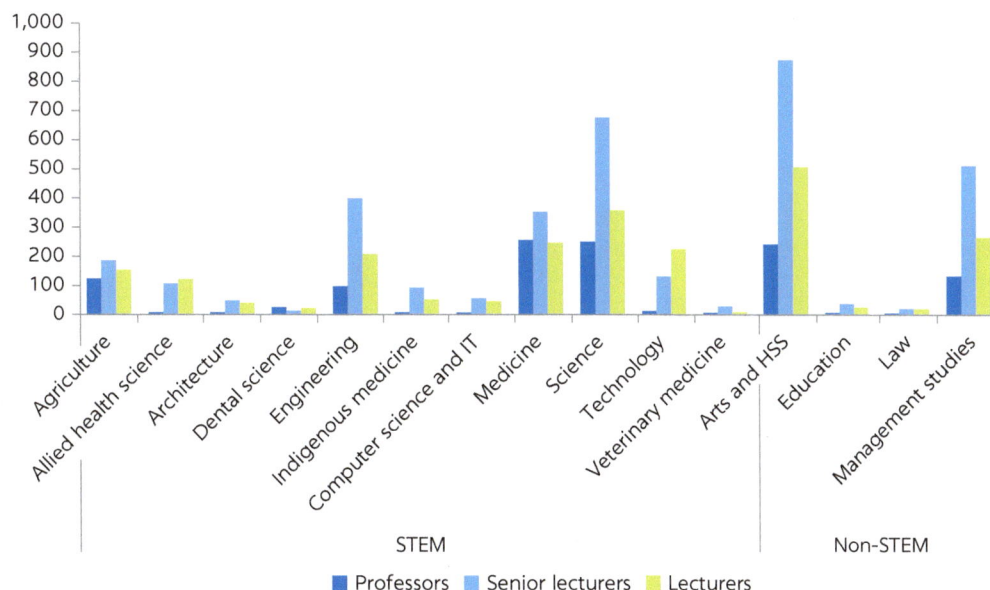

Source: University Grants Commission 2021.
Note: HSS = humanities and social sciences; IT = information technology; STEM = science, technology, engineering, and mathematics.

The academic qualifications of academic staff in state higher education institutions vary by academic stream. In 2021, 29.5 percent of academics in the STEM stream had a PhD, compared with 13.5 percent in the non-STEM stream (figure 3.2).

Student research, publications, and competitions should be encouraged. Research and innovations remain at an early stage in Sri Lanka (Aturupane, Shojo, and Ebenezer 2018). Thus, the research culture in universities needs to be strengthened. Student research and presentations at organized forums encourage critical thinking. Interuniversity competitions are linked to industry or professional bodies to increase interest in the subject area.

Funding is imperative to enhance access to and quality of higher education. Between 2015 and 2021, recurrent spending on higher education increased by 84 percent and capital spending by 54 percent (table 3.6). Total spending increased 73 percent. Spending fell slightly in 2020 due to COVID-19, which led universities to close or offer online learning.

Students can apply for scholarships, with two types of "Mahapola" higher education scholarships available. The top 10 percent of students are eligible for merit scholarships. Ordinary scholarships are awarded based on parents' income. In 2018, merit scholarships were awarded to 1,498 students and ordinary scholarships to 13,490 students—covering 53 percent of students admitted to a university. Students who do not receive a scholarship can apply for a bursary. Parents' income is considered when selecting recipients for a bursary. Scholarships and bursaries, however, are not specifically targeted at STEM education or women.

Students can also get interest-free loans for laptop computers that can be obtained from the Bank of Ceylon and Peoples Bank; by the end of 2018,

FIGURE 3.2

Academic staff in state higher education institutions in Sri Lanka, by STEM and non-STEM stream and qualifications, 2021

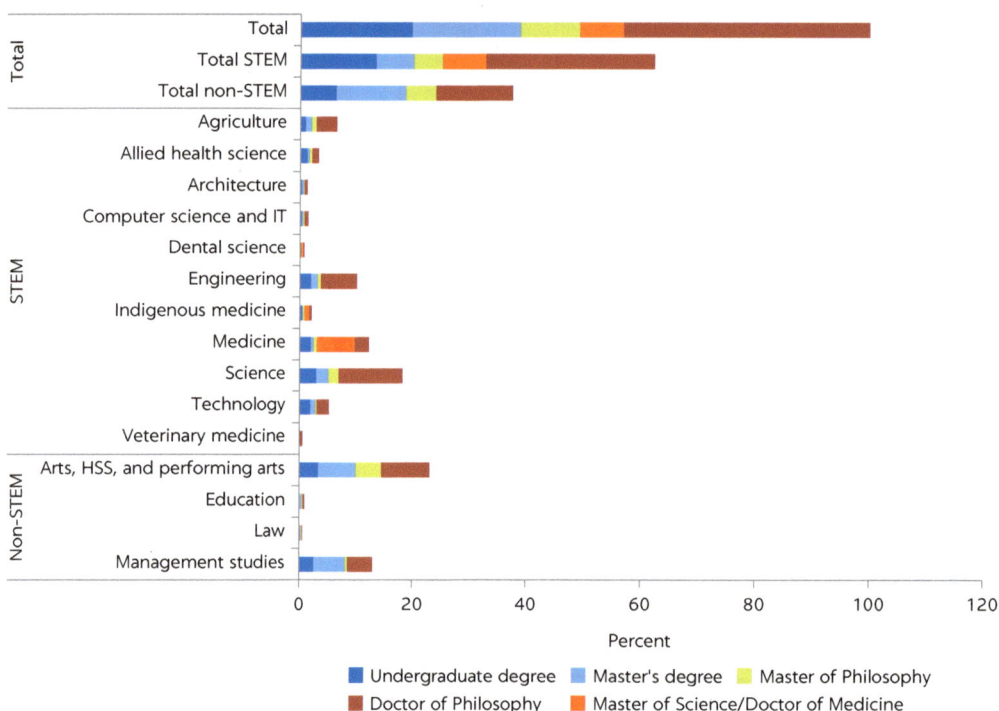

Source: University Grants Commission 2021.
Note: HSS = humanities and social sciences; IT = information technology; STEM = science, technology, engineering, and mathematics.

TABLE 3.6 Spending on state higher education institutions in Sri Lanka, 2021

Millions of Sri Lanka Rupees

TYPE	2015	2016	2017	2018	2019	2020	2021	% INCREASE FROM 2015 TO 2021
Capital	18,099	19,833	20,276	25,538	28,281	25,826	27,902	54
Recurrent	32,071	35,498	38,729	45,823	59,009	57,960	59,120	84
Total	**50,170**	**55,331**	**59,005**	**71,361**	**87,290**	**83,786**	**87,022**	**73**

Source: University Grants Commission 2021.

27,895 students had received such loans. The Ministry of Higher Education provided LKR 96,327,901 to support this program in 2018 and LKR 56,249,159 in 2019.

Career guidance programs in higher education institutions are vital to increase women's participation in the labor force. Career guidance units provide advice on preparing resumes, appearing for interviews, and selecting careers, and job fairs are organized for students.

Access to nonstate higher education intuitions is being encouraged. The government provides interest-free loans of up to LKR 800,000 for students not admitted to a state university who cannot afford a nonstate higher education institute. The Ministry of Higher Education has selected 50 degree courses at 10 nonstate higher education institutes for these degree programs. In 2019, the Bank of Ceylon approved LKR 1,605 million in loans for 2,069 students and paid LKR 593 million in course fees to nonstate higher education institutes for three groups of students. In addition, 2,764 students received interest-free bursary loans for general expenses (Ministry of Higher Education 2019).

FACTORS ENABLING AND PREVENTING LABOR MARKET PARTICIPATION

No laws discriminate against women joining the workforce, and men and women are considered equal in formal work settings. However, specific laws govern women working in factories and mines and at night (World Bank 2021).

Rates of return to secondary and higher education are substantial. Workers with different education qualifications have different rates of return (World Bank 2011):

- GCE O/L qualifications earn returns of 13 percent for men and 21 percent for women.
- GCE A/L qualifications earn returns of 15 percent for men and 18 percent for women.
- University graduates earn returns of 21 percent for both men and women.
- Postgraduate qualifications earn returns of 9 percent for men and 17 percent for women.

The Ministry of Education in charge of science and technology, has taken a leadership role in developing, reviewing, and implementing science and technology policies. The National Science and Technology Commission (NASTEC) is the apex institution for advising on and developing science and technology policies. NASTEC has also set up a Young Scientists Forum to share research findings, issues, and challenges in the sector. Information technology parks, NASTEC, and the Industry Technology Institute are under the State Ministry of Digital Technology and Enterprise Development. The National Science Foundation, National Innovation Agency, and a few other agencies are under SMSDVERI.

Some sectors suffer from worker shortages. There is demand for 21,216 graduate workers, but only 9,076 potential workers are available (Information Communication Technology Agency 2019). Similarly, the demand for manufacturing and engineering workers is 52,363, while the supply is 32,277. Jobs in highest demand include welders and flame cutters, aluminum fabricators, mechanical and maintenance engineering technicians, and electrical engineering technicians.

Professional organizations can help boost female participation. The Institution of Engineers—the premier professional body for engineers—has created one committee for female engineers and another for young engineers. Affinity groups and forums for young engineers have been set up at universities. The Women Engineers Forum has fostered networking, developed members' capacities, and helped communities (Institute of Engineers Sri Lanka 2019). A similar network, WePOWER, has been set up across South Asia for women engineers in the power sector. One of the main goals of this group is to enhance girls' interest in STEM education. According to a baseline assessment in Sri Lanka, 15 percent of technical staff were women (147 of 989 technical staff), including 13 percent of staff of the main utility organization, the Ceylon Electricity Board (CEB) (3,280 of 25,727 staff; World Bank 2020). At CEB in 2019, 25 percent of engineers, 5 percent of supervisors, and more than 75 percent of other workers were women. Women also hold leadership positions in the power sector.

Research, innovation, and university links need to be expanded. A few national research agencies could collaborate with universities to spearhead research in Sri Lanka. These include the National Science Foundation, National Research Council, and NASTEC. In addition, specific discipline-based institutes include the Medical Research Institute, Tea Research Institute, and Rubber Research Institute (Bandara 2020; Esham 2008).

Infrastructure facilities at 33 science and technology organizations are encouraging more scientific, research, and technology work, and the infrastructure can be used by all staff. There are 109 labs in agriculture and veterinary science organizations, 64 in natural sciences, 55 in engineering and technology, and 35 in medical and health sciences (figure 3.3). Other facilities in agriculture and veterinary sciences include plant nurseries, instrument rooms, technical incubators, pest control farms, screening houses, experimental farms, and animal houses.

ICT organizations have been especially active in implementing programs to attract and retain female workers, especially after childbirth (figure 3.4). Business process management firms have programs to attract female workers. In 2019, 1.84 percent of female employees in business process management firms had gone on maternity leave—and 1.59 percent returned to work. Similarly, 4.13 percent of female employees of ICT companies went on maternity leave in 2017, and 3.97 percent returned to work. Management at these firms believes that strategies targeting female workers have helped them to return after maternity leave.

Childcare benefits can reap benefits for employers. Employers can provide childcare benefits to both mothers and fathers at subsidized rates. Employer-supported in-house childcare centers make mothers more productive workers. Employer-supported childcare facilities and benefits encourage women to return to work after childbirth, and the organizations are recognized as being female-friendly. Some companies have a 100 percent maternity

FIGURE 3.3

Infrastructure facilities at science and technology organizations in Sri Lanka

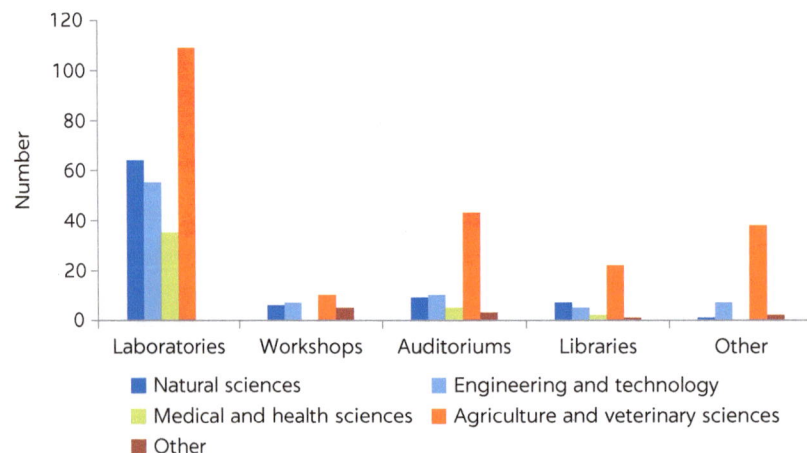

Legend:
- Natural sciences
- Engineering and technology
- Medical and health sciences
- Agriculture and veterinary sciences
- Other

Source: National Science and Technology Commission 2017.

FIGURE 3.4

Strategies implemented to attract and retain female workers in Sri Lanka, by type of organization

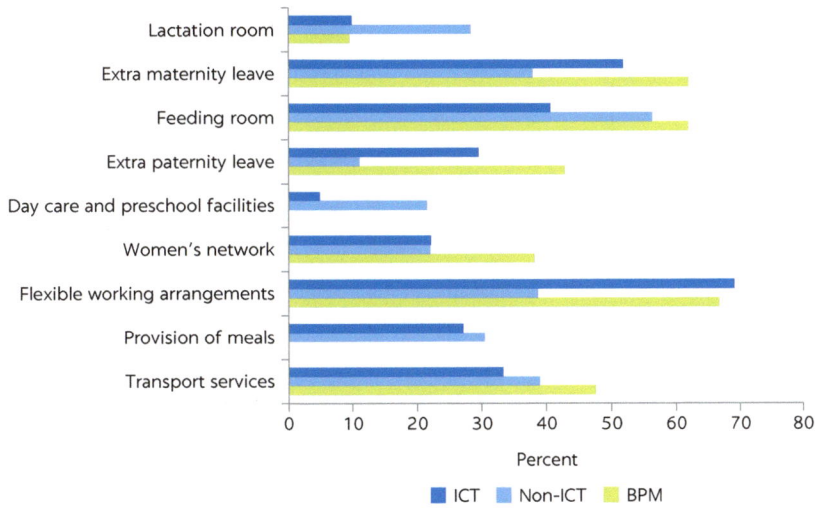

Source: Information Communication Technology Agency 2019.
Note: ICT = information and communications technology;
BPM = business process management firm.

return rate—generating significant business benefits because replacing skilled workers is costly.

Science, technology, and research investments have improved but require further strengthening. Spending by the Ministry of Science, Technology, and Research (formerly the Ministry of Science and Technology) rose from LKR 3,148 million in 2015 to LKR 4,945 million in 2018 (Ministry of Science, Technology, and Research 2015, 2018). This funding supported 10 science, technology, and research institutes as well as science and technology programs organized by the ministry. Between 2015 and 2018, recurrent spending increased by 20 percent and capital spending by 88 percent. In 2018, capital spending included establishing the National Science Center, STEM education development programs in schools, and science promotion programs, as well as providing postgraduate scholarships for PhD degrees, economic development initiatives, and investments in biotechnology parks.

Improving STEM education will raise the Global Innovation Index ranking in Sri Lanka. The country's ranking fell from 89 in 2019 to 101 in 2020 (table 3.7). The Global Innovation Index for Sri Lanka in 2020 comprises rankings of, among other things, institutions (119), human capital and research (119), infrastructure (78), market sophistication (118), business sophistication (70), knowledge and technology outputs (68), and creative outputs (100). The human capital and research component assesses education, tertiary education, and research and development. The infrastructure component focuses on ICT (90), general infrastructure such as electricity (90), and ecological sustainability (39). Institutional and infrastructure facilities need to be improved to facilitate scientific research and innovations. Knowledge and technology outputs include patents, scientific and technical articles, and the like. Creative outputs include assets such as trademarks, industrial designs, organizational models, and creative goods and services.

Sri Lanka has a long way to go to bring STEM education to the levels of some of its neighbors. Most East Asian countries have much higher rankings on

TABLE 3.7 Global innovation indexes in selected South and East Asian countries, 2019 and 2020

REGION	COUNTRY	2019 GLOBAL INNOVATION INDEX	2020 GLOBAL INNOVATION INDEX	INSTITU-TIONS	HUMAN CAPITAL AND RESEARCH	INFRA-STRUCTURE	MARKET SOPHISTICATION	BUSINESS SOPHISTI-CATION	KNOWLEDGE AND TECHNOLOGY OUTPUTS	CREATIVE OUTPUTS	FEMALES EMPLOYED WITH ADVANCED DEGREES	PATENTS	UNIVERSITY AND INDUSTRY RESEARCH COLLABORA-TIONS
East Asia and Pacific	China	14	14	62	21	36	19	15	7	12	n/a	1	29
	Japan	15	16	8	**24**	8	9	10	13	24	24	1	17
	Malaysia	35	33	40	29	48	20	31	38	35	56	63	14
	Republic of Korea	11	10	29	1	14	11	7	11	14	31	1	16
	Thailand	43	44	65	67	67	22	36	44	52	68	60	31
	Vietnam	42	42	63	79	73	34	39	37	38	84	66	65
South Asia	Bangladesh	116	116	124	129	92	100	122	95	115	108	114	121
	India	52	48	61	60	75	31	55	27	64	101	51	45
	Nepal	109	95	114	114	76	40	**58**	102	106	97	92	101
	Pakistan	105	107	99	111	119	116	87	69	108	105	90	46
	Sri Lanka	89	101	119	119	78	118	70	68	100	98	62	73

Source: Cornell University, INSEAD, and World Intellectual Property Organization 2020.
Note: Numbers in bold indicate that the minimum average for the subcomponent was not met at the subpillar or pillar level.

subcomponents of the General Innovation Index than do Sri Lanka and selected South Asian countries. India has the best index in South Asia and the Republic of Korea the best in East Asia—one of the main reasons being their vast investments in human capital and research. In 2020, Sri Lanka's rankings for institutions, human capital and research, market sophistication, and creative outputs were 100 or higher, indicating that they will take a long time to improve. Thus, Sri Lanka should improve factors encouraging research and innovation. Moreover, links between universities and industry should be further strengthened to enhance employment and promote research that helps organizations raise productivity.

Women should be encouraged to submit patent applications. Numbers of patent awards and applications have varied by applicant type (table 3.8). Between 2015 and 2017, the largest share of patents (76 percent) was granted to single inventors, followed by small group collaborations (10 percent). The smallest share went to higher education institutions (2 percent). Similarly, during 2015–17, the most patent applications came from single inventors (76 percent of the total), followed by small group collaborations (about 10 percent); the least came from higher education institutions (2 percent). Single inventors were granted the most patents and submitted the most applications—and women in private and higher education institutions had the fewest. The most common barriers to patent grants and applications were the limited number of research grants or government funding for research, long and complicated approval and application processes, lack of economic incentives and rewards for applications, high application costs, and limited mentors and encouragement by institutions. In addition to these, female scientists cited family care responsibilities as one of the main

TABLE 3.8 **Patent grants and applications in Sri Lanka, by applicant type and gender, various years**

a. Patents granted 2015–17

ORGANIZATION TYPE	TOTAL	MALE	FEMALE
Single inventors	411	325	86
Small group collaborations	56	39	17
Government and semi-government	34	23	11
Private institutions	29	27	2
Higher education institutions	11	10	1
Total	**541**	**424**	**117**

b. Patent applications 2015–17

ORGANIZATION TYPE	2015		2016		2017	
	TOTAL	FEMALE	TOTAL	FEMALE	TOTAL	FEMALE
Single inventors	155	9	199	16	207	19
Small group collaborations	33	10	34	10	32	9
Government and semi-government	15	6	22	4	14	4
Private institutions	13	2	14	1	19	0
Higher education institutions	7	2	5	1	7	3
Total	**223**	**29**	**274**	**32**	**279**	**35**

Sources: Kariyawasam 2018; World Bank calculations.

barriers to engaging in research that leads to patent applications. Moreover, lower representation of women in patenting and intellectual property rights activities indicates gender disparities in university admissions and academic positions in engineering and technology streams.

Science and technology knowledge transfers raise productivity and popularize scientific knowledge in communities. The Ministry of Education has conducted programs to popularize science among various stakeholders. Technology transfer programs are conducted at the 267 Vidatha Centers scattered across the island, which are managed by science and technology officers with science degrees. These programs—targeting entrepreneurs in agriculture, food, chemical, and material-based fields to introduce technology or boost productivity—include mushroom seed production and cultivation, modern yogurt production, and biodegradable packaging. To encourage participation by entrepreneurs, districtwide shops have been opened to market higher-quality products. In addition, quality certificates are issued in collaboration with industrial technology institutes and the Sri Lanka Standards Institution. At the community level, a pilot project has promoted the use of modern, sustainable biomass energy to empower women, make small enterprises more productive, and lower energy costs (Ranasinghe 2018). The main barriers to expanding community-level technology transfers are funding and coordination of grassroots programs, as well as access to modern technology.

Sri Lankan women hold leadership positions in private businesses. In 2018, 59 percent of private companies had one or two female members on their board of directors, 22 percent had three or more, and only 19 percent had all male members (International Finance Corporation 2021). Some firms exhibited gender diversity in leadership positions, and these directors can serve as role models for girls.

Employment outcomes differ based on skill level, region, and gender. Sri Lankan women have higher measured cognitive skills than men, and men and women have the same levels of noncognitive skills (Gunawardena 2015). For men, returns to work experience were strongly associated with higher measured cognitive skills. Most men with lower cognitive skills perform manual labor, and earnings do not increase with experience in such occupations. Women working in urban areas earn 35 percent more than those in rural areas—yet there was no significant difference in earnings for men. The probability of being employed is strongly associated with being married, and having young children reduces the chances of paid employment by 17 percent.

SOCIAL, CULTURAL, AND PSYCHOLOGICAL FACTORS

Many social, cultural, and psychological factors enable and hinder access to and success in STEM education and careers:

- **Media** play a vital role in people's mind-sets. Popular teledramas and films, newspaper stories, and social media articles can encourage students and parents to like or dislike study streams at school and university and influence decisions on whether to join the workforce.
- Most Sri Lankan **parents aspire** to see their children become doctors or engineers. Many role models of doctors appear in mainstream media. But at the cultural level, gender roles are stereotyped, and boys are expected to become

engineers and girls to become doctors or teachers. Parents aspire for their children to complete secondary school to pursue vocational or university education (Himaz and Aturupane 2021). Moreover, parent aspirations and teacher expectations are lower for boys.

- **Parental involvement** is strongly associated with students' intrinsic and extrinsic motivations to learn science and self-efficacy (De Silva, Khatibi, and Azam 2018). In addition, parental involvement varies significantly by income and the type of school category their children attend. However, parental involvement does not differ much in terms of the parents' ethnicity or their children's gender.
- **Parent and student attitudes** toward education influence whether children drop out of school. Poor or ignorant parents also often expect older children to look after younger siblings or engage in child labor, hindering children from attending school. Parents usually expect girls to look after younger siblings (UNICEF 2013). Parents' and children's attitudes toward joining the workforce also influence labor force participation. Most parents encourage sons to work but not daughters.
- **Household per capita income** effects have a positive relationship with education for girls. Among 12-year-old students, the education level of the most educated parent significantly influences math scores for both boys and girls (Himaz and Aturupane 2021), but household per capita income positively affects only girls' scores.
- In addition, **teacher attitudes** significantly influence girls' but not boys' performance.
- In some communities, **early marriage and early cohabitation** practices result in teen pregnancies and dropouts. In 2016, 0.3 percent of girls got married precisely upon turning age 15 (DCS 2017a).
- **Distances to schools, training centers, and workplaces** can influence decisions to stay home. For example, a lack of safe and comfortable transportation to work influences women's decisions to join the workforce (Solotaroff, Joseph, and Kuriakose 2017).
- **Care responsibilities** for young children or older parents can constrain women's labor force participation.
- **Peer pressure** can have negative or positive influences. Peer pressure and bullying keep some children from attending school, particularly boys. Similarly, peer pressure can encourage or discourage girls from joining the workforce.
- **The absence of role models** for boys contributes to boys' underperformance (Aturupane et al. 2018).

REFERENCES

Asian Development Bank. 2020a. *Independent Evaluation Report for Education Sector Development Program.* Manila: Asian Development Bank.

Asian Development Bank. 2020b. *Program Implementation Document for Secondary Education Sector Improvement Program.* Manila: Asian Development Bank.

Aturupane, Harsha, Mari Shojo, and Roshini Ebenezer. 2018. "*Gender Dimensions of Education Access and Achievement in Sri Lanka.*" South Asia Region Education Global Practice Discussion Paper 90. Washington, DC: World Bank. https://openknowledge.worldbank.org/handle/10986/30624 License: CC BY 3.0 IGO.

Bandara, Deepthi C. 2020. "The Sri Lankan Higher Education Journey." In *Handbook of Education Systems in South Asia*, edited by P. Sarangapani and R. Pappu. Singapore: Global Education Systems, Springer. https://doi.org/10.1007/978-981-13-3309-5_65-1.

Cornell University, INSEAD, and World Intellectual Property Organization. 2020. "The Global Innovation Index 2020: Who Will Finance Innovation?" Ithaca, Fontainebleau, and Geneva: Cornell University, INSEAD, and World Intellectual Property Organization.

De Silva, A. D. A., A. Khatibi, and S. M. Ferdous Azam. 2018. "Can Parental Involvement Mitigate 'Swing Away from Science'? Sri Lankan Perspectives." *Cogent Education* 5: 1.

Department of Census & Statistics. 2017a. "Demographic & Health Survey 2016." Colombo.

Department of Census & Statistics. 2017b. "Poverty Indicators: Household Income & Expenditure Survey 2016." Colombo.

Esham, M. 2008. "Research Studies on Tertiary Education Sector—Strategies to Develop University-Industry Linkages in Sri Lanka." NEC, Colombo. http://nec.gov.lk/wp-content/uploads/2014/04/Strategies_to_Develop.pdf.

Gunawardena, D. 2015. *Why Aren't Sri Lankan Women Translating Their Educational Gains into Workforce Advantages?* Washington, DC: Center for Universal Education.

Himaz, R., and H. Aturupane. 2021. "Why Are Boys Falling Behind? Explaining Gender Gaps in School Attainment in Sri Lanka." *World Development* 142 (2021): 105415.

Information Communication Technology Agency. 2019. "National IT-BPM Workforce Survey 2019." Colombo.

Institution of Engineers Sri Lanka. 2019. "E-Newsletter of the Institution of Engineers Sri Lanka." Issue 43. Colombo. http://ioes18.wildapricot.org/article_teambuild.

International Finance Corporation. 2021. *Realizing Sustainability through Diversity: The Case for Gender Diversity among Sri Lanka's Business Leadership*. Washington, DC: International Finance Corporation.

International Labour Organization. 2021. *STEM in TVET: Curriculum Guide: An Initiative of the ILO Women in STEM Workforce Readiness and Development Programme*. Geneva: International Labour Organization. https://www.ilo.org/wcmsp5/groups/public/---ed_emp/---ifp_skills/documents/publication/wcms_776446.pdf.

Kariyawasam, Kanchana. 2018. *Women and IP Commercialization in the Asian Region: Case Study of Sri Lanka*. Geneva: World Intellectual Property Organization. https://www.wipo.int/export/sites/www/women-and-ip/en/docs/women_and_ip_commercialisation_asian_region_sri_lanka.pdf.

Ministry of Education 2012. "Annual School Census." Colombo.

Ministry of Education 2015. "Annual School Census." Colombo.

Ministry of Education 2017a. "Annual Performance Report." Colombo.

Ministry of Education 2017b. "Annual School Census." Colombo.

Ministry of Education 2018. "Annual School Census." Colombo.

Ministry of Higher Education. 2018. "Annual Report." Colombo.

Ministry of Higher Education. 2019. "Annual Report." Colombo.

Ministry of Science, Technology, and Research. 2015. *Annual Performance Report*. Colombo.

Ministry of Science, Technology, and Research. 2018. *Annual Performance Report*. Colombo.

National Science and Technology Commission. 2017. "Science & Technology Status Report of Sri Lanka." Colombo.

Polgampala, A. S. V., H. Shen, and F. Huang. 2016. "Where We Are and Where We Need to Be: Pre Service Science Teacher Preparation in China & Sri Lanka." *American Journal of Educational Research* 4 (16): 1138–44.

Ranasinghe, S. 2018. "From Impoverished to Empowered: Sri Lankan Women Adopt Modern Biomass Technologies." http://www.fao.org/srilanka/news/detail-events/en/c/1150398/.

Solotaroff, Jennifer L., George Joseph, and Anne T. Kuriakose. 2017. *Getting to Work: Unlocking Women's Potential in Sri Lanka's Labor Force*. Washington, DC: World Bank. http://hdl.handle.net/10986/28660 License: CC BY 3.0 IGO.

Sosale, Shobhana, Seo Yeon Hong, Shalika Subasinghe, and Hiran Herat. Forthcoming. *Skills Sector Transformation for Inclusion, Recovery, and Resilience in Sri Lanka.* Washington, DC: World Bank.

Tertiary and Vocational Education Commission. 2019. "Labour Market Information Bulletin." Colombo.

UNICEF. 2013. "Out-of-School Children in Sri Lanka: Country Study." Colombo.

University Grants Commission. 2015. "Annual Report." Colombo.

University Grants Commission. 2021. "Annual Report." Colombo.

World Bank. 2011. *Transforming School Education in Sri Lanka: From Cut Stones to Polished Jewels.* Washington, DC: World Bank. https://documents1.worldbank.org/curated/en/366241468301732117/pdf/660360PUB00PUB0Report0final0version.pdf.

World Bank. 2017. *Sri Lanka—Accelerating Higher Education Expansion and Development Operation Project (English).* Washington, DC: World Bank Group. http://documents.worldbank.org/curated/en/219921486493053365/Sri-Lanka-Accelerating-Higher-Education-Expansion-and-Development-Operation-Project.

World Bank. 2018. *Sri Lanka—General Education Modernization Project.* Washington, DC: World Bank Group. http://documents.worldbank.org/curated/en/480271524967257414/Sri-Lanka-General-Education-Modernization-Project.

World Bank. 2020. "Pathways to Power: South Asia Region Baseline Assessment for Women Engineers in the Power Sector." Energy Sector Management Assistance Program (ESMAP). Washington, DC: World Bank.

World Bank. 2021. *Women, Business and the Law.* Washington, DC: World Bank. http://hdl.handle.net/10986/35094 License: CC BY 3.0 IGO.

World Bank. 2022. *Sri Lanka Development Update: Protecting the Poor and Vulnerable in a Time of Crisis.* Washington, DC: World Bank.

4 Recommendations and Conclusions

FROM EVIDENCE TO ACTION

Interventions to boost access to science, technology, engineering, and mathematics (STEM) education and careers need inputs at various levels—school education, technical and vocational education and training (TVET), higher education, the labor market—over the short and medium to long term. The interventions will require multidisciplinary approaches and coordination with many stakeholders to enhance access, quality, investments, and governance at all levels (Dundar et al. 2017).

PRIMARY LEVEL

- Ensure that all primary schools are fully functioning so that all students, including in remote locations, acquire the foundational knowledge and skills needed for STEM education. If students at the primary level have low attendance levels, schools should conduct investigations to fix the problem.
- Foster and maintain awareness among parents and communities about the importance of compulsory school attendance.
- Ensure that all schools have trained, qualified teachers focused on children's learning outcomes in subjects such as mathematics and the environment. If any students need special attention, coordinate with parents on efforts to improve learning outcomes.
- Review curricula for mathematics and environment subjects to create knowledge of concepts and develop the skills of all students. Activities to impart the proper knowledge should be included in teacher guides for the subjects. Curricula should contain gender-neutral images.
- Develop digital learning materials and promote technology-based tools to facilitate learning.
- Support an inclusive public education system and the investments it requires.
- Have the Ministry of Education and other supporting agencies review and revise policies to facilitate mathematics and environmental studies in all schools.

- In the medium to long term, provide needy children in remote locations with further assistance to enhance school access and quality. Equip all primary schools with the apparatuses required to facilitate mathematics and environmental studies, with enough trained teachers recruited from remote locations.
- Review the School Education Policy to incorporate global trends in improving primary schools.

SECONDARY LEVEL

- Ensure that all secondary schools are fully functioning to provide inclusive access to students, including underprivileged ones. School principals should monitor attendance and encourage students to maintain attendance rates of at least 80 percent.
- Maintain awareness of compulsory school attendance and subjects such as science and mathematics for student development among parents and the community in general.
- Take steps to have qualified and trained teachers in science, mathematics, and practical and technical skills in all secondary schools. In addition, sufficient teachers should be qualified and trained in information and communications technology (ICT), health and physical education, agriculture and food science, and other technology subjects for schools to offer such classes in grades 10 and 11.
- Identify teacher vacancies in science, mathematics, practical and technical skills, and other optional subjects, and fill those vacancies with qualified and trained teachers.
- Enhance teacher training to include subject content training and strengthen teaching styles to improve students' learning outcomes.
- Provide special allowances for teachers in remote locations to encourage teachers to work in them.
- Review strategies for bringing dropouts back to school. Parents and religious and community groups can aid in such efforts.
- Review curricula for science, mathematics, practical and technical skills, and optional subjects and revise them if needed to prepare students for twenty-first-century challenges. Teacher guides will need to be revised and teachers trained to teach the new curricula.
- Supply infrastructure facilities such as science labs, computer labs, and other resources needed to offer science, mathematics, ICT, and other technology subjects. The resources required could include chemicals and utensils to conduct science experiments, as well as computers and the software, equipment, and other items required to offer technology subjects. The status and desired status of infrastructure and other items should be mapped and shortages filled to enhance learning outcomes.
- Enhance the development of digital-based learning materials and provide opportunities to use technology-based tools to facilitate learning.
- Continue to assess science and mathematics knowledge among grade 8 students, and use the resulting data to guide decisions that further strengthen learning outcomes.
- Continue with and offer career guidance programs in grade 9 to enable students to select optional subjects in grades 10 and 11 and, later, for the General Certificate of Education (GCE) for the Advanced Level (A/L).

- Continue to organize regional, national, and international competitions and exhibitions; develop communication materials to disseminate innovations; and so on.
- Invest in an inclusive public education system that provides access to quality learning for all students, paying special attention to lagging regions and underperforming schools.
- Continue school-based leadership and activities and quality assurance activities conducted internally and with the assistance of third parties.
- Promote school-based research and knowledge sharing to disseminate innovations developed and implemented across schools.
- Have the Ministry of Education and supporting agencies review and revise policies to facilitate the teaching of science, mathematics, and optional subjects in all schools.
- Over the medium to long term, review the School Education Policy to incorporate global trends in incorporating STEM-based education concepts.
- Map population growth and enhance facilities in lagging regions to provide access to all students.

COLLEGIATE LEVEL

- Increase the number of type 1AB schools offering science for the GCE A/L, type C schools with the technology stream, and schools offering a vocational stream (especially geared toward STEM).
- Develop and maintain awareness of the importance of selecting STEM subjects for the GCE A/L.
- Monitor attendance and involve parents in increasing it.
- Ensure that all schools have teachers trained and qualified in bioscience, physical science, and technology. Map and fill teacher vacancies.
- Review curricula for bioscience, physical science, and technology subjects to ensure that the curricula provide the knowledge and skills needed for students to pursue higher studies or join the workforce. Changes in curricula should be included in teacher guides, with teachers trained to teach the revised curricula.
- Popularize STEM subjects such as ICT, business statistics, and mathematics among students in the commerce and arts streams.
- Continue developing digital-based learning materials and promote technology-based tools to facilitate learning. Review digital content developed during the COVID-19 pandemic, and consider it supplementary material in the future.
- Offer career guidance programs to highlight options for continued study and the labor market.
- Continue to encourage students to participate in national and international completions
- Review the efficiency of the school system to develop further strategies for supporting and investing in an inclusive public education system.
- Have the Ministry of Education and supporting agencies review and revise policies to facilitate bioscience, physical science, and technology stream subject offerings in all geographic areas.
- In the medium to long term, develop infrastructure facilities—such as buildings and labs—to enhance type 1AB and type C schools. Develop plans to

procure computers and other lab equipment for new buildings in such schools, and recruit and train the number of bioscience, physical science, and technology teachers required in those schools.

TVET INSTITUTIONS

- Increase access to vocational training in STEM areas in public TVET institutions by enrolling more students.
- Continue offering stipends for TVET students in STEM and further encourage female students to pursue STEM.
- Strengthen relationships between skills sector councils and industry to identify occupations suitable for women, develop courses and competency standards, and train teachers.
- Facilitate industry collaborations for apprenticeships, on-the-job training, teacher training, product designs, and innovations in STEM fields.
- Fill teacher vacancies with qualified teachers and continue to provide professional development programs.
- Review and expand the quality assurance system to all TVET institutes.
- Continue to hold annual skills and innovation competitions regionally and island-wide, including female-only segments.
- Strengthen the Sri Lanka Qualification Framework to facilitate TVET students with National Vocational Qualifications (NVQ) to move to NVQ 7, equivalent to a degree.
- Hold awareness sessions for students, parents, and communities that promote female role models and job opportunities.
- Develop inclusive classroom environments in STEM to increase female enrollments and course completion.
- Develop more TVET courses that produce workers for local and international labor markets.
- Strengthen coordination between TVET institutions in all ministries to promote STEM courses, encourage female-friendly content, and develop competencies for the STEM-led world of work.
- Continue to collect student, teacher, and resource information from training institutes to develop a better information management system and generate reports for better decision-making.
- In the medium to long term, consider offering higher stipends to female students following the STEM stream and develop plans to monitor progress in the labor market.

HIGHER EDUCATION INSTITUTIONS

- Increase the number of students enrolled in STEM stream courses by renovating buildings or increasing the use of infrastructure facilities.
- Fill vacancies in university lecturer positions and train lecturers to teach students in STEM areas. Newly recruited academics should also be given funding and opportunities to gain higher research degrees, such PhDs.
- Expand and popularize postgraduate courses in STEM areas.
- Review and revise curricula to integrate content relevant to the world of work and develop the skills of all students. Enhance the content of non-STEM streams by incorporating mathematics and statistics to make such streams more attractive in the labor market.

- Enhance links between universities and industry, and develop a system that encourages university students and academics to file patent applications and register trademarks and technology designs.
- Encourage students and teachers to conduct research, publish scholarly articles, and participate in local and international competitions.
- Offer career guidance for students to join the workforce in the areas they have studied and encourage employment in the private sector, without waiting for the government to provide employment opportunities.
- Provide options for students in the arts stream to take subjects in the STEM stream—perhaps even to earn dual major degrees.
- Encourage nonstate higher education institutions to offer STEM courses, build academic capacity, and increase student assistance.
- Provide opportunities for academics and research students to apply for research grants linked with specific outcomes.
- Continuously enhance funding of state and nonstate universities to increase STEM access and quality.
- In the medium to long term, develop infrastructure facilities such as buildings and labs to increase the number of students enrolled in the STEM streams. State universities can establish new faculties and departments to increase student numbers. The equipment and teachers needed should be planned and resourced so that classes can start as soon as such facilities are ready.
- Develop business links between universities and global businesses or foreign universities to strengthen research and innovation.
- Review the Higher Education Policy to develop universities to raise global rankings of universities in Sri Lanka.

LABOR MARKET

- Review technological and infrastructure developments and work with stakeholder agencies to prepare staff and potential recruits to take up agreed promotion of technological development.
- Promote female role models, including through the media, to encourage schoolchildren and postsecondary students to pursue STEM.
- Advocate recruitment of female workers and development of family- and female-friendly benefits to retain employees after maternity leave.
- Facilitate the creation of childcare centers in the workplace.
- Promote organizational policies to handle sexual harassment issues at the workplace.
- Develop continuous development programs to acquire or enhance STEM skills in the workplace and advance careers.
- Make workplace infrastructure facilities more female-friendly.
- In the medium to long term, review labor market policies and laws to make them more female-friendly, with equal wages for occupations requiring the same knowledge, skills, and abilities.

REFERENCE

Dundar, Halil, Benoit Millot, Michelle Riboud, Mari Shojo, Harsha Aturupane, Sangeeta Goyal, and Dhushyanth Raju. 2017. *Sri Lanka Education Sector Assessment: Achievements, Challenges, and Policy Options*. Washington, DC: World Bank. https://doi.org/10.1596/978-1-4648-1052-7.